THE NEW DESPOTISM

THE NEW DESPOTISM

by

THE RT. HON. LORD HEWART
OF BURY

Lord Chief Justice of England

GREENWOOD PRESS, PUBLISHERS
WESTPORT, CONNECTICUT

Library of Congress Cataloging in Publication Data

Hewart, Gordon Hewart, Baron, 1870-1943.
The new despotism.

Reprint of the 1945 ed. published by E. Benn, London.
1. Administrative law--Great Britain. 2. Great Britain--Executive departments. 3. Executive power--Great Britain. 4. Courts--Great Britain.
I. Title.
KD4879.H48 1975 342'.41'06 75-25259
ISBN 0-8371-8389-8

This edition orginally published in 1945 by Ernest Benn Limited, London

Reprinted with the permission of Ernest Benn, Ltd.

Reprinted in 1975 by Greenwood Press,
a division of Williamhouse-Regency Inc.

Library of Congress Catalog Card Number 75-25259

ISBN 0-8371-8389-8

Printed in the United States of America

PREFATORY NOTE

This little essay is obviously not intended to be more than a brief introduction to a topic of large, and unhappily growing, dimensions. An exhaustive examination of the pretensions and encroachments of bureaucracy—the new despotism—must await greater leisure and another occasion. Yet it seemed to be high time that, at any rate, a note of warning should be offered. *Est quadam prodire tenus, si non datur ultra.*

H.

CONTENTS

CHAPTER I

THE NATURE OF THE QUESTION

Wordsworth begins a well-known poem with the words: "Oh! what's the matter? what's the matter?" A simple and prosaic question like that is not always easy to answer. Nor is it easy to express in a sentence, for the information of Lord Bowen's gentleman on the top of the Clapham omnibus, the precise nature of the present inquiry. Perhaps it may be well to offer at the outset a significant and recent example of the tendency which it is proposed to examine. On the 22nd December 1925 there was added to the Statute-book an Act of Parliament, entitled the Rating and Valuation Act, 1925,[1] which fills ninety pages in the authorized edition of the statutes. It is described as an Act to simplify and amend the law with respect to the making and collection of rates. The marginal heading of section 67 of the Act consists, pleasantly enough, of the words "Power to remove difficulties", and the section provides that if any difficulty arises in connection with the application of the Act to any exceptional area, or the preparation of the first valuation list for any area, "or otherwise in bringing into operation any of the provisions of this Act", the Minister "may by order remove the difficulty". More than that, the Minister may "constitute any assess-

[1] 15 & 16 Geo. V. c. 90.

ment committee, or declare any assessment committee to be duly constituted, or make any appointment, or do any other thing, which appears to him necessary or expedient for securing the due preparation of the list or for bringing the said provisions into operation". Finally, it is provided that "any such order may modify the provisions of this Act so far as may appear to the Minister necessary or expedient for carrying the order into effect". It would be difficult to imagine more comprehensive powers or more remarkable legislation. The Act of Parliament not only in terms empowers the Minister to "do any thing" which he may think expedient for the purpose named, but also in terms empowers him, if he thinks it expedient, to make orders which "may modify the provisions" of the Act of Parliament itself. These far-reaching powers were conferred upon the Minister by the statute for a period of no less than three and a quarter years—that is, until the end of March 1929.

In April 1927 this section was referred to in a case [1] which came before a Divisional Court of the King's Bench. The details of the case need not be repeated. The question turned upon an order made by the Minister under the Act approving a scheme for an assessment area, to which objection was taken on the ground that the constituent authorities were entitled to decide among themselves on the size or number of the assessment committee and on the mode of representation of their own group. In the result the Court held that, in the particular case,

[1] *The King* v. *Minister of Health: ex parte Wortley Rural District Council*, 1927. 2 K.B. 229.

there had been no usurpation or excess of jurisdiction. In the judgement, however, which expressed the unanimous opinion of the Court, the following passage with reference to section 67 of the statute is to be found (at p. 236):

> "This, I think, though I say it with some hesitation, may be regarded as indicating the high-water mark of legislative provisions of this character. It is obvious that if this Court had taken another view of the case presented to us to-day and had decided to quash this order as having been made *ultra vires*, the Minister might to-morrow, under the provisions of section 67, have arrived at the same end by making an order and removing the difficulty."

Now it will probably be admitted that matters must have gone rather far before a Minister thought fit to propose, and Parliament, either deliberately or by inadvertence, consented to approve, a scheme that empowered a Government department, on grounds of expediency, to make departmental orders modifying the provisions of the statute which conferred the power. A little inquiry will serve to show that there is now, and for some years past has been, a persistent influence at work which, whatever the motives or the intentions that support it may be thought to be, undoubtedly has the effect of placing a large and increasing field of departmental authority and activity beyond the reach of the ordinary law. Whether this influence ought to be encouraged, or whether it ought rather to be checked and limited, are questions into which, for the moment, it is not necessary to enter. But it does at least seem desirable that the influence itself should be clearly discerned, that its essential nature and tendency should be quite plainly exhibited, and that its various methods and manifestations should not be allowed to continue and multiply under a cloak of obscurity. The citizens of a State may indeed believe or boast that, at a given moment, they enjoy, or at any rate possess, a system of representative institutions, and that the ordinary law of the land, interpreted and administered by the regular Courts, is comprehensive enough and strong enough for all its proper purposes. But their belief will stand in need of revision if, in truth and in fact, an organized and diligent minority, equipped with convenient drafts, and employing after a fashion part of the machinery of representative institutions, is steadily increasing the range and the power of departmental authority and withdrawing its operations more and more from the jurisdiction of the Courts.

In order to perceive clearly the nature of this influence or tendency, and the relation in which it stands to the essential foundations of the Constitution, it may be well to examine briefly, first, the meaning and implications, on the one hand, of the Rule of Law, and, on the other hand, of the Continental system of so-called "Administrative Law" with which the Rule of Law is sharply contrasted. The apologists of the growing system, or lack of system, which it is here proposed to explore sometimes permit themselves to speak of it as if it were "Administrative Law". But the description, it will be seen, is quite curiously the reverse of the truth. The Continental system of

"Administrative Law", profoundly repugnant as it is to English ideas, is at least a system. It has its Courts, its law, its hearings and adjudications, its regular and accepted procedure. It would be a strange misuse of terms if the name of "Administrative Law" were to be applied to that which, upon analysis, proved to be nothing more than administrative lawlessness.

Let nobody be so foolish or so flippant as to suppose that any attack is here intended upon what it is a commonplace to describe as the best Civil Service in the world. In a treatise upon photography, as somebody says, one may assume the existence of the sun. In remarks upon the mischiefs of bureaucracy one may assume the excellence of the Civil Service. Yet it may perhaps be well to remember that high capacity and ardent zeal never need to be more carefully watched than when they appear to have entered, with all their might, upon a wrong road. It does not take a horticulturist to perceive that, if a tree is bearing bad fruit, the more vigorously it yields the greater will be the harvest of mischief. Many persons of course have from time to time perceived and deplored this particular mischief. But, somehow, some of them have found it more convenient to their inclinations or their aims to refrain from words even of good omen. They have passed by, like the prudent Levite, on the other side. Or they have been content to say that, "after all, people get the kind of government they deserve", wholly refusing to recognize the power of a skilful and organized minority. Or, again, they have so nicely balanced their appreciation of what is good and their examination of what is less good that, with the convenient help of a little confusion of thought, they have left the detached spectator wondering upon which side they appeared. But to the impartial eye of the fearless citizen it is obvious that the official just as surely seeks to escape the jurisdiction of the Courts when he takes power to make regulations having the force of a statute as when he in terms provides that his decisions shall not by any method be open to review. It is no less obvious that, if such an endeavour were the isolated act of an ingenious individual, its consequences might be almost trivial. But other considerations apply if a mass of evidence establishes the fact that there is in existence a persistent and well-contrived system, intended to produce, and in practice producing, a despotic power which at one and the same time places Government departments above the Sovereignty of Parliament and beyond the jurisdiction of the Courts. If it appears that this system springs from and depends upon a deep-seated official conviction, which in turn it nourishes and strengthens by each successive manifestation of its vigour, that this, when all is said and done, is the best and most scientific way of ruling the country, the consequences, unless they are checked, must be in the highest degree formidable.

That there is in existence, and in certain quarters in the ascendant, a genuine belief that Parliamentary institutions and the Rule of Law have been tried and found wanting, and that the time has come for the departmental despot, who shall be at once scientific and benevolent, but above all a law to himself, needs no demonstration. There is an agreeable story, not too old, of a distinguished Anglo-

Indian civilian, who, returning home on leave after a prolonged absence, passed the Houses of Parliament on his way from Victoria to Charing Cross. "What place is that?" he asked. "That, sir," was the answer, "is Parliament—the Houses of Parliament." "Really," he exclaimed, though his exclamation was in fact slightly different, "does that rubbish still go on?" Everybody knows the frame of mind, and everybody has met some of the teachers in that school. But another aspect of the matter is illustrated by a well-known conversation which took place, not so many years ago, between a distinguished Treasury official, if the epithet is not tautologous, and the Chancellor of the Exchequer. It happened that matters had not gone quite smoothly in the House of Commons that evening. The departmental specialist was not, for once, able to say to his chief, after the rising of the House, with that air which as nearly approaches a tone of triumph as official decorum permits, "Well, sir, we have got our clauses". What he did say was that he wondered whether all this palaver was really necessary. After all, what was the good of the House of Commons? And how perfectly useless was the House of Lords! Why should the work of the expert be always at the mercy of the ignorant amateur? Why should people be allowed to try to govern themselves when it was manifestly so much better for them to be governed by those who knew how to govern? "Seriously," he asked, "could not this country be governed by the Civil Service?" "Undoubtedly it could," replied the Chancellor of the Exchequer, "undoubtedly it could. And I am quite sure that you and your colleagues would govern the country remarkably well. But let me tell you this, my young friend: at the end of six months of it, there would not be enough lamp-posts in Whitehall to go round."

The matter has, no doubt, its humorous side. Yet many persons may think that it has not only a serious side, but a seriousness which goes far beyond what might at first blush be supposed. It is not merely that in this instance Parliament is being out-manœuvred, or that in that instance the Courts have been defied. It is that the whole scheme of self-government is being undermined, and that, too, in a way which no self-respecting people, if they were aware of the facts, would for a moment tolerate. Much nonsense, to be sure, is written about what is called democracy. It might be thought, on the testimony of some of its apologists, that democracy was a patent medicine—on the testimony of others that it was a fancy religion. But when once the fact is appreciated that democracy is really the name of a form of government, the essence of which is that every citizen in the State shares the responsibility for the good government of the State, and when it is further understood that, in the opinion of many competent observers, by no means confined to this side of the Atlantic alone, the great achievement and the enduring pride of our history and institutions are precisely to have exhibited to the world, in an unexampled way, the art and practice of real self-government, as well in peace as in war, the true dimensions of the present issue, and the true nature of the assault which is being resisted, become reasonably clear. Much toil, and not a little blood, have been spent in bringing slowly into being a polity wherein the people make their laws, and independent judges administer them. If that edifice is to be overthrown, let the overthrow be accomplished openly. Never let it be said that liberty and justice, having with difficulty been won, were suffered to be abstracted or impaired in a fit of absence of mind.

The paradox which is in course of being accomplished is, indeed, rather elaborate. Writers on the Constitution have for a long time taught that its two leading features are the Sovereignty of Parliament and the Rule of Law. To tamper with either of them was, it might be thought, a sufficiently serious undertaking. But how far more attractive to the ingenious and adventurous mind to employ the one to defeat the other, and to establish a despotism on the ruins of both! It is manifestly easy to point a superficial contrast between what was done or attempted in the days of our least wise kings, and what is being done or attempted to-day. In those days the method was to defy Parliament—and it failed. In these days the method is to cajole, to coerce, and to use Parliament—and it is strangely successful. The old despotism, which was defeated, offered Parliament a challenge. The new despotism, which is not yet defeated, gives Parliament an anaesthetic. The strategy is different, but the goal is the same. It is to subordinate Parliament, to evade the Courts, and to render the will, or the caprice, of the Executive unfettered and supreme. The old King, as Rudyard Kipling sings in "The Old Issue", sometimes reappears under a new name:

> All we have of freedom, all we use or know—
> This our fathers bought for us long and long ago.

Ancient Right unnoticed as the breath we draw—
Leave to live by no man's leave, underneath the Law.

. . . .

Over all things certain, this is sure indeed,
Suffer not the old King: for we know the breed.

. . . .

Howso' great their clamour, whatsoe'er their claim,
Suffer not the old King under any name!

It is pleasant to observe the excuses which are from time to time put forward by the apologists of bureaucratic encroachment. One of the most ingenious of them has lately expressed his opinion in the following way. "Provided", he says, "that matters of principle and of substance are reserved for Parliament itself, provided that (as is usually the case with vigilant and well-organized interests) those concerned have been consulted in advance, provided that the Minister can be called to account for any wrongful or excessive exercise of his powers, and provided that full publicity can be secured, then the system of departmental legislation has advantages of elasticity, promptness, and technical knowledge which may be set against the dangers of encroachment by the Executive upon the citizen's liberty." The accumulation of successive provisos in this carefully constructed plea may be thought to be interesting and instructive. The strength of a chain is the strength of its weakest link. How, it may be asked, if matters of principle or of substance are not reserved for Parliament itself? How if those concerned (and as a rule the public is concerned) have not been consulted in advance? And how if full publicity cannot be secured until the mischief has been done? As for the proviso that "the Minister can be called to account for any wrongful or excessive exercise of his powers", two reflections at least are unavoidable. One is that prevention is better than cure, and indescribably better than mitigation. The other is that experience has shown too often what precisely the process of calling the Minister to account may be worth. What with the collective responsibility of Ministers, and the inexorable demands of the party system, once the mischief has been done, the whole force of the Parliamentary majority tends to be directed, not so much to undoing it, as to preventing a defeat in a Parliamentary division. "This is our lobby", say the Whips, when the critical moment comes, and at the eleventh hour the private member is naturally disposed to acquiesce. Here, as elsewhere, it seems to be important to distinguish things which are different from each other. It is one thing to confer power, subject to proper restrictions, to make regulations. It is another thing to give those regulations the force of a statute. It is one thing to make regulations which are to have no effect unless and until they are approved by Parliament. It is another thing to make regulations, behind the back of Parliament, which come into force without the assent or even the knowledge of Parliament. Again, it is a strong thing to place the decision of a Minister, in a matter affecting the rights of individuals, beyond the possibility of review by the Courts of Law. And it is a strong thing to empower a Minister to modify, by his personal or departmental order, the provisions of a statute which has been enacted. De Lolme said indeed that Parliament could do everything but make a man a woman or a woman a man. There are those who think that it has now, to some extent, accomplished even that feat. But what would De Lolme have said to the suggestion that Parliament should enact that a particular individual should have power, at his pleasure, to override its enactment?

An agreeable writer, collecting from the pages of Boswell and elsewhere individual opinions expressed by Samuel Johnson, has compiled and composed a kind of Johnsonian creed or soliloquy, which sums up concisely the essence of his faith. If a similar method were applied to the ardent bureaucrat, the amateur of the new despotism, his reflections might perhaps be indicated in some such creed as this:

1. The business of the Executive is to govern.
2. The only persons fit to govern are experts.
3. The experts in the art of government are the permanent officials, who, exhibiting an ancient and too much neglected virtue, "think themselves worthy of great things, being worthy".
4. But the expert must deal with things as they are. The "foursquare man" makes the best of the circumstances in which he finds himself.
5. Two main obstacles hamper the beneficent work of the expert. One is the Sovereignty of Parliament, and the other is the Rule of Law.
6. A kind of fetish-worship, prevalent among an ignorant public, prevents the destruction of these obstacles. The expert, therefore, must make use of the first in order to frustrate the second.
7. To this end let him, under Parliamentary forms, clothe himself with despotic power, and then, be-

cause the forms *are* Parliamentary, defy the Law Courts.

8. This course will prove tolerably simple if he can: (*a*) get legislation passed in skeleton form; (*b*) fill up the gaps with his own rules, orders, and regulations; (*c*) make it difficult or impossible for Parliament to check the said rules, orders, and regulations; (*d*) secure for them the force of statute; (*e*) make his own decision final; (*f*) arrange that the fact of his decision shall be conclusive proof of its legality; (*g*) take power to modify the provisions of statutes; and (*h*) prevent and avoid any sort of appeal to a Court of Law.
9. If the expert can get rid of the Lord Chancellor, reduce the judges to a branch of the Civil Service, compel them to give opinions beforehand on hypothetical cases, and appoint them himself through a business man to be called "Minister of Justice", the coping-stone will be laid and the music will be the fuller.

Yet in observing the bureaucratic encroachments—the manifestations of the new despotism—of recent years, especially under the greater latitude encouraged and bequeathed by the War, it is necessary to beware of a common fallacy. It is natural and usual enough when the acts of any body of men, or of any association or organization, are being considered—as, for example, a Government, a Cabinet, a party, a Committee, or a newspaper—to assume that that which has been done is a true reflection of the intentions and the wishes of every individual member of the association. But this assumption is not always correct. It may well be that, in the particular circumstances, responsibility in relation to third parties must be shared by all and can be escaped by none. Yet, if all the facts were known, it might often appear that, within the body which was being criticized, there was a sincere minority, whether large or small, whose opinions tended rather to coincide with the opinions of the critic himself, and who were habitually engaged, behind the scenes, in combating, in preventing, and in reducing, at any rate, the dimensions of the kind of mischief under consideration. So when the performances of the new despotism are under review, it is natural enough to employ such a phrase as "the Government departments". But it would be strange indeed if they were all cut after the same pattern, or if everybody comprised within them were of the same mind. Nobody who is at all aware of the facts would dream of entertaining any such view. There can be no doubt, for example, that the Law Officers of the Crown, the Treasury solicitor, and the Parliamentary draftsman have from time to time used all their influence to prevent, or to mitigate, acts which they could not approve. In a sense the fact is welcome. But it has a formidable aspect as well. If in truth and in fact the things which are done exhibit only the resultant force derived from influences that are to some extent in conflict, it follows that the force which makes directly in favour of those things is strong indeed. Such, there can be little doubt, is the force of the new despotism in Whitehall.

CHAPTER II

THE RULE OF LAW

It seems convenient to retain the expression the "Rule of Law", especially as it has become perfectly well known to more than one generation of Englishmen. But the expression itself is not free from ambiguity. It is often used, for example, in the sense in which a particular proposition, or statement of legal doctrine, is described as being a "rule of law". But that of course is not the sense in which it is used here. What is meant here by the "Rule of Law" is the supremacy or the predominance of law, as distinguished from mere arbitrariness, or from some alternative mode, which is not law, of determining or disposing of the rights of individuals. It is, or at any rate it was until quite recently, a commonplace to say that the "Rule of Law" is one of the two leading features which distinguish our Constitution. So it has been ever since the eleventh century, and, if this leading feature or essential characteristic is to be diminished or destroyed, it seems at least desirable that the work of diminution or demolition should be openly and frankly performed, with the British public standing by, fully instructed and deliberately consenting. Nothing could well be more unfortunate than that a change of so fundamental a character should be brought about piecemeal, by subterranean methods, which might escape general observation until the mischief had been carried to completion.

Professor Dicey, in his classical work on the "Law of the Constitution", enumerates three distinct yet kindred conceptions which are involved in the statement that the English Constitution is characterized by the supremacy, or the rule, of law. The statement means, first, that in England no man can be punished, or can be lawfully made to suffer either in his body or in his goods, except for a distinct breach of law established in the ordinary legal manner before the ordinary Courts. It means, secondly, that in this country not only is no man above the law, but every man, whatever his rank or condition may be, is subject to the ordinary law of the land and the jurisdiction of the ordinary Courts. And, finally, it means that the general principles of our Constitution are mainly the result of judicial decisions determining the rights of private persons in particular cases brought before the Courts.

There is probably at this time of day little need to expound the meaning, or to dwell upon the importance, of these essential principles. Englishmen indeed are so thoroughly accustomed to them as to take them for granted. They have become a second nature. They are, so to say, part of the bracing air we breathe. They exemplify, as they spring from, that love of justice, and respect for it, which have excited witnesses from other countries, like Tocqueville and Voltaire, for example, to tributes so manifestly sincere,—a love of justice which in its turn is closely bound up with the unchanging passion for self-government. The underlying contrast, the permanent antithesis, is between the supremacy of the law on the one hand and, on the other hand, the arbitrary, which may easily prove to be the capricious, exercise of lawless power. Nothing perhaps is more profoundly repugnant to the English mind than that authority should be irresponsible or uncontrolled, that it should operate at pleasure or in the dark, that men should live in an atmosphere of uncertainty as to the nature of the rights they enjoy or the penalties to which they are exposed, or that among fellow-citizens there should be one code for one class of persons and a different code for others.

> "With us", as Professor Dicey says,[1] "every official, from the Prime Minister down to a constable or a collector of taxes, is under the same responsibility for every act done without legal justification as any other citizen. The Reports abound with cases in which officials have been brought before the Courts, and made, in their personal capacity, liable to punishment, or to the payment of damages, for acts done in their official character but in excess of their lawful authority. A colonial governor, a secretary of state, a military officer, and all subordinates, though carrying out the commands of their official superiors, are as responsible for any act which the law does not authorize as is any private and unofficial person."

But the supremacy of Law, as we know it, means something more than the exclusion of arbitrary power, and something more also than the equality of all citizens before the ordinary law of the land administered by the ordinary Courts. It means that in this country, unlike some foreign

[1] *Law of the Constitution*, 8th Edition, p. 189.

countries, the principles of the Constitution are, in Dicey's phrase, inductions or generalizations based upon decisions pronounced by the Courts as to the rights of particular individuals. Under the contrasted system, where the Constitution is written out in declarations or definitions of rights, the rights of the individual may be said to be deductions drawn from the principles of the Constitution. The contrast is vital and is to be traced to profound differences of history, of temperament, and of outlook. This is not the place for any comparison of the respective merits and advantages of the two systems. But it may at least be observed that, under the system which we know, it is far more difficult for constitutional rights to be suspended or taken away.

To summarize the matter, it may be said that the "Rule of Law" comprehends and denotes the following principles:

1. No one can lawfully be restrained or punished, or condemned in damages, except for a violation of the law established to the satisfaction of a judge or jury or magistrate in proceedings regularly instituted in one of the ordinary Courts of Justice. The rights of personal liberty and of freedom of speech, the liberty of the press, and the right of public meeting, are all a result of the application of this fundamental principle.

2. Everyone, whatever his position, Minister of State or Government official, soldier or policeman, is governed by the ordinary law of the land and personally liable for anything done by him contrary to that law, and is subject to the jurisdiction of the ordinary Courts of Justice, civil and criminal.

The plea of "act of State" is not permissible as a defence to an action in respect of anything done within the realm, or to any action by a British subject. It is confined to proceedings commenced by foreigners in respect of duly authorized acts done by officers or servants of the Crown abroad.

The Crown—that is to say, the Government—cannot itself be proceeded against, either by petition of right or otherwise, for any alleged wrong on the part of its servants. The remedy for any such wrong is against the individual wrongdoer. But in practice the Crown as a general rule pays any damages that may be recovered against its servants for wrongful acts committed in the course of their public employment.

3. No one who is charged with a violation of the law can effectively plead, either in a civil or in a criminal Court, that his act was done in obedience to the command of a superior, even the command of the King himself. The maxim "The King can do no wrong" imports not only that the King cannot be proceeded against for any alleged wrong, but also that he cannot authorize any wrongful act so as to justify the wrongdoer.

The right of personal liberty is the right not to be arrested or detained or otherwise subjected to physical restraint except in accordance with the law. And to speak generally, that is to say, except in the case of persons who are not *sui juris*, or persons subject to military law, the law recognizes an arrest or any sort of physical restraint as justifiable only where the person restrained is suspected of having committed a crime and is arrested in order that he may be brought before the Court for trial, or where he has been convicted of a crime and sentenced to imprisonment.

The law affords three remedies by means of which this right of personal liberty may be vindicated: (1) by the writ of habeas corpus, (2) by an action of damages for false imprisonment, and (3) by a prosecution of the person imposing the illegal restraint—that is, a prosecution for assault.

The writ of habeas corpus is a very ancient common law writ, which now issues from the High Court of Justice, directed to any person detaining another, commanding him to produce the body of the person detained before the Court, showing the day and the cause of his detention, to be dealt with as the law requires. The writ accordingly enables any person who is alleged to be unlawfully detained or imprisoned to be actually produced before the Court, and the cause of his detention inquired into. Unless a legal justification for his detention is shown, the Court will then order his immediate release. The writ is granted *ex debito justitiae*, and may be issued not only during term but also during vacation by any judge of the High Court. It will be issued on the application either of the prisoner himself or of any person who satisfies the Court or judge that there is *prima facie* ground for believing that the prisoner is unlawfully detained. The remedy is open not only to British subjects, but also to foreigners imprisoned within the realm. If the writ is disobeyed by the person to whom it is directed, he is liable to be attached for contempt of Court.

The Habeas Corpus Act of 1679, which applies only to

persons detained on a criminal charge, contains provisions to meet various devices by which the common law right to the writ had been evaded, and to secure that the prisoner shall in suitable cases be admitted to bail and in any case be promptly tried, and imposes heavy penalties for the refusal of the writ and for disobedience to it.

At various times, in periods of political unrest, statutes have been passed enabling persons to be arrested on suspicion of treasonable practices and certain other offences, and detained without bail or trial. Measures of this kind do no doubt to a limited extent suspend temporarily the operation of the Act of 1679. But these statutes, though they have been called "Habeas Corpus Suspension Acts", have not in any sense suspended the general right to the writ of habeas corpus, nor have they legalized any arrest or imprisonment which would not have been otherwise lawful. Hence it is that such statutes have nearly always been followed by Acts of Indemnity, protecting from liability persons who acted in pursuance of the Suspension Acts.

The right of freedom of speech, again, is simply the right which everyone has to say, write, or publish what he pleases so long as he does not commit a breach of the law. If he says or publishes anything with a seditious intention, or speaks blasphemous words or publishes any blasphemous writing, he is guilty of a misdemeanour for which he may be prosecuted and punished. If he publishes anything merely by word of mouth which is untrue and defamatory of an individual, he may be sued by the person defamed for damages in an action of slander; and if he publishes defamatory matter by writing, print, or in some other permanent form, he may either be sued in a civil action for damages or be prosecuted criminally for the libel, and in a prosecution the truth of the libel does not constitute a defence unless it is in the public interest that the truth in regard to the matter should be known. It is also a misdemeanour to speak or publish words defamatory of any Court of Justice, or of the administration of the law therein, with intent to obstruct or invalidate its proceedings, or diminish its authority and dignity and lower it in public esteem. Subject to these conditions, any person may say, write or print, and publish anything he thinks fit without risk, and fair comment or criticism in regard to a matter of public interest is no libel.

A seditious intention is defined by statute (60 Geo. III. & 1 Geo. IV. c. 8, s. 1) as an intention to bring into hatred or contempt the person of His Majesty, his heirs or successors, or the government and constitution of the United Kingdom as by law established, or either House of Parliament, or to excite His Majesty's subjects to attempt the alteration of any matter in Church or State as by law established, otherwise than by lawful means. On a prosecution for sedition the defendant will be conclusively presumed to have intended the natural consequences of his words or acts, and it is therefore sufficient if his words or acts have a tendency to produce any of the consequences so stated. But it must be remembered that all such prosecutions are tried with a jury, who are entitled to return a general verdict of guilty or not guilty, and therefore determine the question of the criminality or innocence of the words used by the defendant. It is now extremely seldom that any attack on the Government or on either House of Parliament is treated as seditious, and the Constitution is frequently abused with impunity. In the absence of a tendency to cause riot or rebellion, or to disturb the peace of the Kingdom, the greatest latitude is permitted in the discussion of political affairs.

The liberty of the press is similarly a mere application of the principle that no one is liable to be punished or condemned in damages except for a breach of the law. Under recent statutes newspapers have certain privileges relating to the publication of fair and accurate reports, published contemporaneously, of proceedings in Courts of Justice, and of public meetings, and the publication at the request of any Government department, Commissioner of police, or chief constable of any notice or report issued for the information of the public. And, in an action for a libel in a newspaper, it is competent for the defendant to plead as a defence that the libel was published without actual malice and without gross negligence and that a full apology was published as soon as possible, provided that such plea is accompanied by a payment into Court in satisfaction for the libel. Further, no criminal prosecution can be commenced against any person responsible for the publication of a newspaper for any libel published in it, until the order of a judge in chambers has been obtained, the person charged to have notice and an opportunity of being heard against the application.

With these exceptions persons responsible for publications in the press are subject to precisely the same liabilities, civil and criminal, and the same jurisdiction and course of procedure, for any libellous, seditious, or blasphemous matter in their publications as if it were published in any other way.

In like manner, there is not in the British Constitution any such thing recognized as a definite right of public meeting. The right is the result of individual rights of personal liberty and freedom of speech, which are themselves the result of an application of the principle of the Rule of Law. In other words, the right of a number of people to assemble together in a lawful manner for public discussion or other lawful purposes is simply an aggregation of the rights of each of the members of the assembly to go where he pleases so long as he does not break the law, as, for instance, by committing a trespass or causing an obstruction to a highway, and to say what he pleases provided it be not seditious, blasphemous, or defamatory.

An assembly may be unlawful either because of the purposes for which it is held or because of the manner in which it is held. For instance, an assembly of three or more persons is an unlawful assembly if they are assembled with intent to commit a breach of the peace; and an assembly of three or more persons with intent to carry out any common purpose, whether lawful or unlawful, is an unlawful assembly if it is held in such a manner as to give people in the neighbourhood reasonable grounds to apprehend a breach of the peace in consequence of it. But a public meeting, if otherwise lawful, does not become unlawful merely because it is prohibited by a Secretary of State or magistrate, or by the police.

If an unlawful assembly has actually begun to execute

the purpose for which it is held by a breach of the peace and to the terror of any member of the public, it becomes a riot.

An unlawful assembly may lawfully be dispersed by force even though it has not yet become a riot, and all persons taking part in the assembly can be prosecuted for misdemeanour. It is justifiable, not only for magistrates, soldiers, and the police, but also for all citizens to use whatever force may be necessary to put down riots and breaches of the peace. Indeed, it is the duty of all citizens, if called upon, to take part in the suppression of riots and the prevention of breaches of the peace.

The position of the soldier, that is to say, any person, officer or private, who is subject to military law, is that, while he is subject to special duties and liabilities and to the jurisdiction of special tribunals under military law, he is also at all times subject to the duties and liabilities of an ordinary citizen, and to the jurisdiction of the ordinary Courts. If he commits a crime under the ordinary law he may be tried in the ordinary Criminal Court (referred to in the Army Act as a "Civil Court"), though, except in the case of murder, manslaughter, and certain other serious crimes, he is also liable to be tried by court-martial. For purely military offences he can be tried only by court-martial.

If a soldier is acquitted or convicted by a civil Court, he cannot afterwards be tried for the same offence by court-martial, but an acquittal or conviction by a court-martial is no bar to a subsequent indictment in a civil Court for the same offence. If, however, he has been sentenced to punishment by the court-martial, the civil Court, in awarding punishment, must have regard to any military punishment already undergone.

When a person is charged in a civil Court with any crime under the ordinary law, the fact that he was acting in obedience to superior orders is not of itself a defence, although under military law he is bound to obey such orders. In such cases any serious injustice may be prevented by the exercise of the right of the Attorney-General, as representing the Crown, to enter a *nolle prosequi*, or by means of the prerogative of pardon.

No person who is not subject to military law is liable to be tried by court-martial, and it is for the civil Courts to determine in any given case whether a person is or is not subject to military law. Any excess of jurisdiction on the part of a court-martial can be prevented by the writs of prohibition, certiorari, and habeas corpus, and officers who, as members of such a court, do acts not authorized by law, are liable to civil proceedings for damages, or to criminal proceedings, according to the nature of the case.

Private soldiers and non-commissioned officers of the regular forces are not liable to be taken out of His Majesty's service by any process, execution, or order of any Court of Law, or to be compelled to appear in person before any Court of Law, on account of any debt, damages, or sum of money not exceeding £30. Nevertheless a person who has a cause of action against a soldier may proceed to judgement and execution, though not to execution against the person, pay, or military equipment of the defendant. Subject to this special exemption, officers and soldiers are in the same position as civilians with regard to the liability to be sued in the ordinary Courts for debts and civil wrongs.

Nobody can weigh and consider a summary statement of this kind without observing two main facts. The first is that the crucial decisions are the decisions of the Courts. The second is that the Courts which are referred to are the ordinary Courts. It makes not merely some difference but all the difference that under our Constitution, which is said to have grown and not to have been made, which—in other words—is the accumulated result of particular decisions and not the sudden product of a general declaration, there is not one Court for the constitutional problem and another Court for the controversy between individual citizens, not one Court for the official and another Court for litigation to which no official is a party, but one and the same Court for all parties and for all suits. To this topic it will be necessary, presently, to return. But it is of no less vital and far-reaching importance that the order which determines the question is the order of a Court. All that is involved and implied in the term "Court" is essential. It may well be that, in a particular case, a perfectly correct opinion might be obtained from some anonymous person, incapable of identification, who heard none of the parties to the controversy, but brought his individual reason to bear in private upon a miscellaneous bundle of correspondence. It is even possible that, in a particular case, a mysterious individual of that kind might not be in the smallest degree tempted or diverted from a sound opinion by the fact, if it happened to be the fact, that he was closely associated with one of the parties to the controversy. But it is manifest that an opinion so arrived at differs by the whole width of the heavens from the decision of a Court. The work of a Court involves many important ingredients, as for example, (1) that the judge is identified and is personally responsible for his decisions; (2) that the case, subject to rare exceptions, is conducted in public; (3) that the result is governed by the impartial application of principles which are known and established; and (4) that all parties to the controversy are fully and fairly heard. In other words, the decision of a Court is in every important respect sharply contrasted with the edict, however benevolent, of some hidden authority, however capable, depending upon a process of reasoning which is not stated and the enforcement of a scheme which is not explained. The administration of the law of the land in the ordinary Courts presupposes, at least, personal responsibility, publicity, uniformity, and the hearing of the parties.

CHAPTER III

"ADMINISTRATIVE LAW"

Between the "Rule of Law" and what is called "administrative law" (happily there is no English name for it) there is the sharpest possible contrast. One is substantially the opposite of the other.

In order to exhibit the true nature of this contrast between the "Rule of Law" and "administrative law", each of which in its turn will hereafter be contrasted with administrative lawlessness, it may be convenient first to consider "administrative law" in outline and afterwards more particularly to examine some of its features. In France and in most other European continental countries a system of "administrative law" exists. It is known in France as "droit administratif". It is a system which is fundamentally opposed to the English conception of the "Rule of Law", especially as regards exemption from the jurisdiction of the ordinary legal tribunals, in the case of public officials acting in performance or purported performance of their official duties. In countries where this system of administrative law prevails the rights and obligations of all servants of the State, and also of all private individuals in relation to servants of the State acting in their official capacity, as well as the procedure for enforcing those rights and obligations, are governed by special rules which are, in general, administered by special tribunals, and the principles underlying these rules differ essentially from the principles forming the basis of the law which governs the relations of private individuals towards one another. Under this system, the ordinary Courts of Justice are regarded as having no jurisdiction to deal with any dispute affecting the Government or its servants, all such disputes being within the exclusive cognizance of the administrative Courts, the chief of which, in France, is the *Conseil d'État*. This Council was originally a purely administrative body, and though its composition has varied at different periods of French history, and it has gradually become more judicial in character, the members have always held office at the pleasure of the Government of the day.

Where, in the course of a case in an ordinary Judicial Court, it appears that a question of administrative law is involved, the Court is bound to refer the matter to the Council of State for decision. Where it is doubtful whether a question of administrative law is or is not involved, a conflict of jurisdiction arises. Until 1872 it was for the Council of State itself to determine all such questions of jurisdiction, the Council thus having, in effect, the power to fix the limits of its own jurisdiction. By a law of 1872 a Conflict-Court was established to decide questions of conflict of jurisdiction as between the administrative and the judicial Courts. This Conflict-Court consists of nine members. Three members are elected by the Judges of the Court of Cassation, which is the highest Judicial Court in France, from among themselves. Three members are elected by the Council of State, also from among themselves. Two members are elected by the above-named six members of the Conflict-Court, one of whom is usually a Judge of the Court of Cassation, and the other a member of the Council of State. The Minister of Justice, a member of the Government, is *ex-officio* President. The eight elected members hold office for three years, but may be, and usually are, re-elected. The Minister of Justice does not often attend the sittings of the Court, though he may do so when the Court is equally divided. A Vice-President, chosen by the Court from among its own members, usually presides. In France a public official is not answerable in any Court, even an administrative Court, for what is regarded as an act of State, however unjustifiable his conduct may have been according to the ordinary law of the land. And agents of the Government are exempted from punishment for any act of interference with the liberty or rights of citizens, if the act was done in obedience to the orders of a superior. On the other hand, damages may be recovered from the State itself, through the Council of State, for unlawful acts of agents of the Government.

"Administrative Law", therefore, properly so called, whatever else may be said or thought about it, is at any rate a form or branch of law. The essential idea which underlies and gives meaning to "droit administratif" is not that State officials, in their official dealings with private citizens, are above the law, or are a law unto themselves. It is rather that the position and liabilities of State officials, and the rights and liabilities of private individuals in their dealings with officials as such, form a separate and distinct chapter of law, which depends upon principles different, indeed, from the principles of the ordinary law, but nevertheless legal principles. Nor is it that the rights and liabilities of private individuals in their dealings with officials as such are matters which are beyond or beneath the reach of established legal procedure. It is rather that for these matters a special procedure is provided, which has its own Courts, its own cases, its own precedents, and its own methods. An examination of the history of the topic during the last century and a quarter shows indeed some remarkable developments in the direction, not at all of extending, but always of limiting and curtailing the peculiar authority of "droit administratif", and of rendering that which was once administrative more and more judicial in character. Yet the fact remains that at no time was the judicial element absent. The special Courts were associated, in ways in which the ordinary Courts were not, with the administration. But they were nevertheless Courts, which heard and determined the matters in issue.

If one starts with the assumption that the Government, and every one of its servants, enjoys as such a special class of rights and privileges as against private individuals, and that the nature and extent of those rights and privileges are to be determined upon principles which differ from the principles of the ordinary law, it follows naturally enough that suitable steps should be taken in order to prevent either the Government or the ordinary Courts from trespassing upon the other's territory. It is in that sense that the expression "separation of powers" is used in countries where "droit administratif" is familiar. It means of course that, while the Judges in the ordinary Courts ought to be independent of the Executive, the Government and its officials ought to be free from the jurisdiction of the ordinary Courts. But the phrase, like so many other phrases, is often misused. In a country like our own, where the notion of "droit administratif" serves only by way of comparison and contrast, for the reason that the thing itself is completely opposed to the first principles of our Constitution, the "separation of powers" refers, and can refer only, to the principle that the Judges are independent of the Executive. Yet the phrase is sometimes employed, by the apologists of administrative lawlessness, for the purpose of suggesting, by means of a confusion of ideas, that here also the Government and its officials, while they are amenable to the jurisdiction of no other Courts, are or ought to be free from the jurisdiction of the ordinary Courts.

In France, therefore, it is not surprising to find administrative Courts, having their defined subject-matter, existing side by side with ordinary or "Common Law" Courts, having their defined subject-matter also. Nor is it surprising that, for the purpose of ousting the jurisdiction of the ordinary Courts, recourse has been had from time to time to the expedient of raising a conflict (*élever un conflit*), that is, of taking the point that the question in issue could not be determined by the ordinary Court without encroachment upon the province of the administrative Court.

In other words, rightly understood, "droit administratif" is a definite system of law, the rules and principles of which, it is true, differ essentially from the rules and principles of the ordinary law governing the relations of private citizens *inter se*. Nevertheless, it is a system of true "administrative law", administered by a tribunal which applies judicial methods of procedure. The Council of State, when it is exercising judicial as distinguished from administrative functions, acts by a Committee which is in many respects analogous to the Judicial Committee of the Privy Council, in the exercise of its jurisdiction to hear appeals from the Dominions and in Prize Causes. The tribunal considers the arguments of advocates and delivers reasoned judgements. Those judgements are reported, and form precedents from which a fixed system of legal rules has been evolved. In short, the system may aptly be described as a special branch of the law for the determination of questions of a particular kind, and the tribunal as a quasi-judicial tribunal for administering that special branch of law.

CHAPTER IV

ADMINISTRATIVE LAWLESSNESS

It is not, but it ought to be, common knowledge that there is in this country a considerable number of statutes, most of them passed during the last twenty years, which have vested in public officials, to the exclusion of the jurisdiction of the Courts of Law, the power of deciding questions of a judicial nature. Usually the power is given nominally to the Minister or other head of a Government department, sometimes to the department itself, and it is commonly provided that his or its decision shall be final and conclusive.

When it is provided that the matter is to be decided by the Minister, the provision really means that it is to be decided by some official, of more or less standing in the department, who has no responsibility except to his official superiors. The Minister himself in too many cases, it is to be feared, does not hear of the matter or the decision, unless he finds it necessary to make inquiries in consequence of some question in Parliament. The official who comes to the decision is anonymous, and, so far as interested parties and the public are concerned, is unascertainable. He is not bound by any particular course of procedure, unless a course of procedure is prescribed by the department, nor is he bound by any rules of evidence, and indeed he is not obliged to receive any evidence at all before coming to a conclusion. If he does admit evidence, he may wholly disregard it without diminishing the validity of his decision. There is not, except in comparatively few cases, any oral hearing, so that there is no opportunity to test by cross-examination such evidence as may be received, nor for the parties to controvert or comment on the case put forward by their opponents. It is, apparently, quite unusual for interested parties even to be permitted to have an interview with anyone in the department. When there is any oral hearing, the public and the press are invariably excluded. Finally, it is not usual for the official to give any reasons for his decision.

To employ the terms administrative "law" and administrative "justice" to such a system, or negation of system, is really grotesque. The exercise of arbitrary power is neither law nor justice, administrative or at all. The very conception of "law" is a conception of something involving the application of known rules and principles, and a regular course of procedure. There are no rules or principles which can be said to be rules or principles of this astonishing variety of administrative "law", nor is there any regular course of procedure for its application. It is possible, no doubt, that the public official who decides questions in pursuance of the powers given to his department does act, or persuades himself that he acts, on some general rules or principles. But, if so, they are entirely unknown to anybody outside the department, and of what value is a so-called "law" of which nobody has any knowledge?

The idea of justice contemplates at least an independent

and impartial judge, who founds his judgement on evidence and reason. By a provision of the Act of Settlement the Judges hold office during good behaviour, instead of, as before, at the pleasure of the Crown, and they can be removed only on an address to the Crown by both Houses of Parliament. They are, therefore, practically irremovable, and it may be observed that their salaries, being charged on the Consolidated Fund, do not appear in the annual votes. Moreover, by Parliamentary practice, it is not permitted to comment on the conduct of a Judge except on a formal resolution for an address to the Crown for his removal.

The system of so-called administrative "law" in this country has little or no analogy to the "droit administratif" of the Continent, and is an indescribably more objectionable method. The "droit administratif" is administered by real tribunals, known to the parties, and these tribunals apply definite rules and principles to the decision of disputes, and follow a regular course of procedure, though the rules and principles applied are different from those of the ordinary law governing the relations of private citizens as between themselves. Moreover, the tribunals give reasons for their decisions and publish them. In a word, the "administrative tribunals" of the Continent are real Courts, and what they administer is law, though a different law from the ordinary law. More than that, the "droit administratif" is a regular system of law, applicable not only to all matters pertaining to the public service, but also to all disputes between the Government or its servants on the one hand and private citizens on the other hand.

Administrative "law" in this country is not really a system at all, but is simply an exercise of arbitrary power in relation to certain matters which are specified or indicated by statute, not on any definite principle, but haphazard, on the theory, presumably, that such matters are better kept outside the control of the Courts, and left to the uncontrolled discretion of the Executive and its servants.

The public official is not independent. As a civil servant, he is liable to be dismissed at any time without notice, and without any enforceable right to compensation. One would have thought it perfectly obvious that no one employed in an administrative capacity ought to be entrusted with judicial duties in matters connected with his administrative duties. The respective duties are incompatible. It is difficult to expect in such circumstances that he should perform the judicial duties impartially. Although he acts in good faith, and does his best to come to a right decision, he cannot help bringing what may be called an official or departmental mind, which is a very different thing from a judicial mind, as everybody who has had any dealings with public officials knows, to bear on the matter he has to decide. More than that, it is his duty, as an official, to obey any instructions given him by his superiors, and, in the absence of special instructions, to further what he knows to be the policy of his department. His position makes it probable that he should be subject to political influences.

Let it be supposed, for the sake of the argument, that the power of deciding disputes as to liability to income-tax were vested in the Board of Inland Revenue, without appeal to the Courts. Could it be suggested that the subject would be likely to receive judicial treatment? "Oh," it may be said, "but that is an extreme case which would never be sanctioned by Parliament." Yet it would not be different in principle from the case exhibited by the powers vested in the Minister of Health in relation to National Insurance. It is the decision of his delegate which is final and conclusive, both in fact and in law, as to the rates of contribution payable by or in respect of insured persons, and his findings of fact are conclusive on any question whether any employment or class of employment falls within the scope of the Act,—a question which, of course, determines the liability to pay contributions.

Will anybody at this time of day deny that it is essential to the proper administration of justice that the decision should be based on evidence, and that the evidence should be heard in the presence of both parties, who are given the opportunity of cross-examination? Evidence not tested by cross-examination is nearly always misleading and practically valueless. The public official, as has been observed, may, and often does, decide without any evidence at all, and he may act on *ex parte* statements, made by one party without anything to support them, which are never brought to the knowledge of the other party, so that he has no opportunity to controvert them. Is it too much to say that such proceedings are a mere travesty of justice? It is also essential to the proper administration of justice that every party should have an opportunity of being heard, so that he may put forward his own views and support them by argument, and answer the views put forward by his opponent. More than that, it is of great importance that all judicial proceedings should be held in public, so that the public may know what is being done, and be able to judge whether it is really justice, or injustice, that is being administered, and also have a guide to their own conduct. The departmental policy of secrecy, which is inveterate, is in itself sufficient to condemn the system under which the public departments act as tribunals to decide disputes of a judicial nature. This secrecy naturally leads to the conclusion that the departments are afraid of their proceedings being made public, and tends to destroy confidence in the fairness of their decisions. How is it to be expected that a party against whom a decision has been given in a hole-and-corner fashion, and without any grounds being specified, should believe that he has had justice? Even the party in whose favour a dispute is decided must, in such circumstances, be tempted to look upon the result as a mere piece of luck. Save in one or two instances, none of the departments publishes any reports of its proceedings, or the reasons for its decisions, and as the proceedings themselves, if any, are invariably held in secret, even interested parties have no means of acquiring any knowledge of what has taken place, or what course the department is likely to take in future cases of the same kind that may come before it. A departmental tribunal is, however, in no way bound, as a Court of Law is, to act in conformity with previous decisions, and this fact is commonly regarded as one of the reasons for the policy of secrecy. Others may think that the department is afraid to disclose inconsistencies and a want of principle in its decisions. However that may be, the policy is fatal to the placing of any reliance on the impartiality and good faith of the tribunal. It is a queer sort of justice that will not bear the light of publicity.

In the kind of "legislation" which is being considered, it is usual to provide that the decision of the Minister shall be final and conclusive. When this is the case, the Courts are powerless to intervene, however unjust and absurd a decision may appear to be, and even though it is obviously based on an erroneous view of the law. It may be said that, if it can be shown that no real discretion was exercised by the deciding official, and the decision is merely capricious, or is perverse or corrupt, the Courts might hold it void on the ground that it does not really constitute an exercise of the authority vested in the Minister at all. But where one is dealing with a decision given without reasons, by an anonymous official, who is not ascertainable, how can any such matter be proved? How can it be shown that such a person, who has not disclosed the evidence, if any, on which he purported to act, was prompted by any particular motives? How can it be determined whether he has acted in good or bad faith, when he has not stated the reasons for his decision? It may be that the decision is apparently so perverse that the party against whom it is given has a reasonable suspicion that it was dictated by spite or vindictiveness, or was even corrupt. But, without knowing who the deciding official is, it is of course impossible for a person aggrieved to prove anything of the kind, or even to furnish grounds for suspecting it. The victim is, in such a case, perfectly helpless, and entirely without remedy. He is completely at the mercy of a person who, for all he knows, may be a bureaucratic tyrant. If he did attempt to challenge the decision by proceedings in a Court of Law, he might well be told by the Court that it must be presumed that the Minister acted in good faith, and in such circumstances the presumption is irrebuttable.

It may be said that there is no substantial ground for the fear of unfairness or corruption in the Civil Service. As to unfairness, people who have had disputes with public officials may sometimes conceivably hold a contrary opinion. As to corruption, that is a vice from which the Service is completely and undoubtedly free. It is of vital importance that it should so continue. But if there were any great extension of the system of giving uncontrolled and arbitrary powers to public officials, it is as certain as that night follows day that corruption might creep in. We might then be cursed with the corrupt bureaucrat. The bureaucratic despot we already have. To take a simple instance, the treatment of the panel doctors under the National Health Insurance Acts is pure despotism. The doctors are liable, at the mere discretion of the official who acts for the Minister of Health, to be ruined professionally by being struck off the panel, or, as a lesser punishment, to be fined to an arbitrary extent. In one instance, a fine of £1000 was imposed on two doctors who carried on business in partnership. "Excessive prescribing", an offence wholly unknown to the law, which consists in prescribing for the patient medicines that are either too expensive in quality or too liberal in quantity, is one of the things for which a doctor may be penalized. One might think that, for a person who is bound by law to insure and pay contributions under the Acts, the best medicine ought to be prescribed in illness. But apparently that is not always the view of the department. One might wonder whether, in this matter, the interests of the patients are adequately taken into consideration.

It is sometimes enacted that, before the Minister comes to a decision, he shall hold a public inquiry, at which interested parties are entitled to adduce evidence and be heard. But that provision is no real safeguard, because the person who has the power of deciding is in no way bound by the report or the recommendations of the person who holds the inquiry, and may entirely ignore the evidence which the inquiry brought to light. He can, and in practice, sometimes does, give a decision wholly inconsistent with the report, the recommendations, and the evidence, which are not published or disclosed to interested individuals. In any case, as the official who decides has not seen or heard the witnesses, he is as a rule quite incapable of estimating the value of their evidence. So far, therefore, as restraining the arbitrary power of the deciding official is concerned, the requirement of a public inquiry is in practice nugatory, and it cannot be of much value in enabling him to form a just conclusion. It seems absurd that one official should hold a public inquiry into the merits of a proposal, and that another official should be entitled, disregarding the report of the first, to give a decision on the merits.

It is indeed sometimes suggested that these arbitrary powers are given by Parliament, who would not confer them in cases where it is considered that they are likely to be abused. But that is only theoretically true. In existing conditions the Cabinet, as representing the Government of the day, is, generally speaking, the real legislative power, Parliament merely confirming its proposals, and there can be little doubt that it is the officials in the departments concerned who initiate the legislation by which the arbitrary powers are conferred upon them. When Parliament passes such legislation, one may wonder how many members outside the Ministry know what they are really doing. How much less do the people know what is being done in this respect by their representatives! It is inconceivable that such legislation would be passed, at all events without protest, if the legislators knew that they were sapping the foundations of the Constitution. All great constitutional lawyers have recognized that it is the rule, or supremacy, of the law, administered by independent judges, that is the basis of all our constitutional liberties, and it is this characteristic of the British Constitution which, above all, makes that Constitution admired throughout the civilized world. Arbitrary power is certain in the long run to become despotism, and there is danger, if the so-called method of administrative "law", which is essentially lawlessness, is greatly extended, of the loss of those hardly won liberties which it has taken centuries to establish.

One of the marks of despotism, as all history shows, is that it is unteachable. Its intrinsic nature, it would seem, is such that it must always, sooner or later, express itself in ways which are not only indefensible but also quite manifestly indefensible. The fact is not, perhaps, to be regretted. If it were otherwise, despotism might have more dupes, and a longer run. As it is, it exhibits itself, sooner or later, in a fashion which has the effect of exciting public observation, so that despotism is checked for a time, and has to start again. Attention has already been directed to a statute of the year 1925 (the Rating and Valuation Act, 1925) which contained the egregious provision that the Minister might, if he thought fit, actually modify the provisions of the Act itself. That provision was piloted through both Houses of Parliament. But it did not escape remark. On the contrary, since it became law, it has on many occasions been the subject of criticism, not only in public speeches and writings, but also in the Law Courts. It might have been thought that the amateurs of the new despotism, unless they regarded public opinion with complete indifference, and unless they were also satisfied that they could count upon perfect complaisance or utter inattention in both Houses of Parliament, would avoid, at any rate for a time, the repetition of that particular revelation of themselves. But what followed? In the early part of 1929 a new Local Government Bill was introduced which contained a clause (originally clause 111) in the following terms:

> "If any difficulty arises in connection with the application of this Act to any exceptional area, or in bringing into operation any of the provisions of this Act, the Minister may by order remove the difficulty, or make any appointment, or do any other thing which appears to him necessary for bringing the said provisions into operation, and any such order may modify the provisions of this Act so far as may appear to the Minister

> necessary or expedient for carrying the order into effect."

Here, then, was another proposal to enact that the Minister, if he thought it necessary, or even expedient, might by order "modify the provisions" of the enactment. The House of Commons did not like it. A good deal of water had flowed under the bridges, and a good many remarks had been made, in public and in private, some of them Parliamentary, and some of them less Parliamentary, between 1925 and 1929. A storm, or at least a sort of storm, arose, and the Minister found it expedient, or even necessary, to promise amendment. But the amendment, when it came, was something quite wonderful. After a good deal of criticism, the amended clause, polished and pruned, was added to the Bill, and emerged from the House of Commons, in the following form (the clause now being numbered 120):

> "If any difficulty arises in connection with the application of this Act to any exceptional area, or in bringing into operation any of the provisions of this Act, the Minister may make such order for removing the difficulty as he may judge necessary for that purpose, and any such order may modify the provisions of this Act," and so on as before.

That is to say, the words "by order remove the difficulty, or make any appointment, or do any other thing which appears to him necessary for bringing the said provisions into operation" were taken out, and in their place the following words were inserted: "make such order for removing the difficulty as he may judge necessary for that purpose", while the power to modify the provisions of the Act remained. Such was the official redemption of the promise given to the House of Commons to meet by amendment the objection which had been taken. Did ever a mountain in labour bring forth a more ridiculous mouse? "The difference between the two clauses is", as the *Law Journal* truly said (February 23, 1929) "a case of Tweedledum and Tweedledee. In fact, the practical effect is the same, and the Minister has found it impossible to carry out his undertaking, and yet leave the clause in being." Nor is it to be supposed that either the Minister himself, or any of the skilled advisers upon whom he depended, was not perfectly well aware of the exiguous nature of the change. The House of Commons, it was believed, for some reason or other, would ultimately acquiesce, even though for a time it protested. What is significant in this transaction, it may be suggested, is the frame of mind of those who drafted and approved the original proposal, and had the courage to put forward the amendment as removing the objection to it.

The sequel is not without interest. When the measure reached the House of Lords, the clause had come to be clause 123. In the discussion on the previous clause in Committee (March 8, 1929) something had been said upon the provisions for laying before Parliament certain orders and regulations made under the Act. "We may be told", said Lord Strachie, "that we can have confidence in the present Minister of Health. I quite agree, but the present Minister of Health will not always be there, and we may have a Minister who will adopt a very hostile attitude towards County Councils and local bodies and want to centralize everything in Whitehall. There is always that danger, and we must look ahead." When clause 123 was reached, no amendment was proposed to the first part of the clause, which provided, in the terms already set out, for the making of orders that might "modify the provisions of this Act". The attack, such as it was, was directed against the second part of the clause, which provided merely that "every order made under this section shall be laid before Parliament as soon as may be after it is made". Lord Askwith moved an amendment for the purpose of adding the words, "and shall not be of any effect unless and until a Resolution affirming the order is passed by each House of Parliament". The amendment, he said, "would give a control to Parliament which has rather been before the country, and which the country desires, against orders being made by a Minister without anybody else having any control". The amendment was afterwards withdrawn upon an assurance given by the Lord Chancellor. "I am quite willing," Lord Hailsham said, "if your Lordships think it right, that any exercise of the power of clause 123 should be brought to the special attention of Parliament by providing that, instead of its merely being laid on the Table, and subject to disallowance by a Resolution under clause 122, in the case of an order made under clause 123 there should be the necessity for its confirmation by an affirmative Resolution within a named number of days after Parliament meets, after the order has been made." The last phase was reached on the Report Stage in the House of Lords (March 14,

1929). Again the first part of the clause, giving power to make orders modifying the provisions of the Act, was allowed to remain in the form in which it had come from the House of Commons. But the second part of the clause, by the combined result of more than one amendment, was altered so as to read in the following way:

> "Every order made under this section shall come into operation upon the date specified therein in that behalf, but shall be laid before Parliament as soon as may be after it is made and shall cease to have effect upon the expiration of a period of three months from the date upon which it came into operation, unless at some time before the expiration of that period it has been approved by a resolution passed by each House of Parliament:
>
> "Provided that, in reckoning any such period of three months as aforesaid, no account shall be taken of any time during which Parliament is dissolved or prorogued, or during which both Houses are adjourned for more than four days."

It is in that form that the clause now appears as section 130 of the Local Government Act, 1929. From all of which it will be seen (1) that the power to modify, by departmental order, the provisions of the Act, remains; (2) that every such order is to come into operation upon the date specified in the order in that behalf; (3) that the period of three months runs from the date so specified; and (4) that the proviso with regard to the reckoning of that period, although to the careless reader it might seem to involve an extension of the period of Parliamentary control, in effect extends the period during which the order may be in operation without Parliamentary approval.

It may be observed that *The Times*, in a leading article in its issue, dated the 16th February 1929, said with reference to this clause, enabling the Minister by Order to modify the provisions of the statute:

> "The true precedents, it has been pointed out, must be sought further back than 1888. They are the pretensions to the dispensing powers under the Stuarts and the Statute—obsequiously passed by both Houses—which declared that anything enacted by King Henry VIII. or by Order in Council should have the force of law."

CHAPTER V

THE SYSTEM AT WORK

During recent years a practice has grown up, and is rapidly being extended, whereby Parliament delegates to the public departments more or less wide powers of legislation. In consequence of the increasing demand of the departments for legislation giving them the detailed control of matters connected with local government, health, education, industry, housing, and so forth, Parliament is, it is said, overburdened, and quite incapable of dealing adequately and in detail with the subject upon which it is invited to legislate. The words "in consequence of the increasing demand of the departments for legislation" may be used advisedly, because the public may probably think that there is too much legislation, and also that there are too many public officials. It is interesting to notice that the growth of the system of subordinate legislation by the departments has proceeded side by side with a great increase in the number of public officials.

There are various forms of departmental legislation. Sometimes Parliament passes an Act expressing its intention in general terms, and leaving the mode of carrying out that intention to be settled by rules and regulations to be made by the public department which is charged with the supervision of the matters legislated upon. Sometimes the department is given power to make orders having the force of law with reference to the subject-matter of the statute. And in some cases the department is empowered, within limits, to repeal or vary the express provisions of the Act conferring the powers.

For instance, by section 1, sub-section (2), of the Road Transport Lighting Act, 1927 (17 & 18 Geo. V. c. 37), the Minister of Transport may exempt, wholly or partially, vehicles of particular kinds from the requirements of the Act, and by sub-section (3) he may, by regulations, add to or vary such requirements.

Again, by section 1 of the Trade Boards Act, 1918 (8 & 9 Geo. V. c. 32), the Minister of Labour may, by special order, extend the provisions of the Trade Boards Act, 1909, to new trades, or withdraw any trade from the operation of that Act, and may alter or amend the Schedule to the Act. By section 2 (1) of the Act of 1918 a special order so made is to have effect as if enacted in that Act.

There are recent instances of the power of modifying the provisions of the enabling Act which has been given for the purpose of removing difficulties in bringing the Act into operation, two of which are as follows:

The Unemployment Insurance Act, 1920 (10 & 11 Geo. V. c. 30), by section 45 provides:

> "If any difficulty arises with respect to the constitution of special or supplementary schemes or otherwise in any other manner whatsoever in bringing this Act into operation, the Minister (of Labour), with the consent of the Treasury, may by order do anything which ap-

pears to him necessary or expedient for the constitution of such schemes or otherwise for bringing this Act into operation, and any such order may modify the provisions of this Act so far as may appear necessary or expedient for carrying the order into effect."

By the Rating & Valuation Act, 1925 (15 & 16 Geo. V. c. 90), section 67 (1), to which reference has already been made:

> "If any difficulty arises in connection with the application of this Act to any exceptional area, or the preparation of the first valuation list for any area, or otherwise in bringing into operation any of the provisions of this Act, the Minister (of Health) may by order remove the difficulty, or constitute any assessment committee, or declare any assessment committee to be duly constituted, or do any other thing which appears to him necessary or expedient for securing the preparation of the list or for bringing the said provisions into operation, and any such order may modify the provisions of this Act so far as may appear to the Minister necessary or expedient for carrying the order into effect."

The extent to which the Courts of Law have jurisdiction to review and question the validity of statutory rules and orders depends, of course, upon the terms of the statute which gives the power to make them, and from which their force is derived. Sometimes such rules and orders are, as they manifestly ought to be, liable to be challenged on the ground that they are not within the powers of the authority making them, or, in other words, that they are *ultra vires*, or on the ground that in making them the authority did not exercise the discretion vested in it, but took into consideration extraneous matters.

The usual means whereby the Courts secure that the departments shall not legislate in abuse of their powers is by the prerogative writs of prohibition or certiorari, which are issued by the King's Bench Division of the High Court. By the writ of prohibition a department which is proceeding with the consideration of a statutory rule or order in excess of its powers, may, before the rule or order is made, be prohibited by the Court from proceeding further in the matter. And by the writ of certiorari the department may be commanded to bring into Court a rule or order after it is made, so that it may be reviewed, and, if it is found to be *ultra vires*, or if it is found that the department took extraneous matter into consideration, may be quashed.

Sometimes the enabling statute provides that the rule or order shall be laid before Parliament for a certain number of days, and, if it is objected to during that time by resolution of either House, shall be annulled. But such a provision does not prevent the Court from inquiring into the validity of the rule or order, and, if it is found to be invalid on either of the grounds above mentioned, from quashing it, either before or after the expiration of the period during which it is before Parliament. But, provided that a rule or order is not invalid on the ground that it is *ultra vires*, or on the ground of extraneous matter having been taken into consideration, the Court has no jurisdiction to review it on its merits, or to inquire into the soundness of the discretion exercised by the legislating department. The Court can prevent a department from acting illegally, but cannot require it to act reasonably.

Where delegated legislation is subject to judicial control, it is perhaps not open to the most serious kind of objection. But various forms of words have been used in connection with this sort of legislation in order to limit the controlling power of the Courts, and in some instances, where private rights are seriously interfered with, the jurisdiction of the Courts has been entirely ousted, and the officials in the exercise of their powers have been rendered wholly free from judicial control.

Sometimes it is provided that the Minister (an expression which, of course, means some official in his department) may make such orders as he shall think fit, apparently with the view of indicating that he is intended to have a very wide discretion, and of preventing the Court from interfering with any order, whatever its terms, relating to the matter concerning which he is given power to legislate.

So, for example, section 10 of the Roads Act, 1920 (10 & 11 Geo. V. c. 72), provides that—

> "Where any persons are, whether by virtue of any Act or otherwise, liable to pay any sums, by way of mileage charges or other annual payments, in respect of the use of any road by their vehicles, the Minister (of Transport) may, on an application by those persons in that behalf, and after considering any objections made by any person interested, suspend, modify, or determine the liability to make the payments, as he shall think fit."

So, again, by section 6 (5) of the London Traffic Act, 1924 (14 & 15 Geo. V. c. 34), the Minister of Transport may, on an appeal, make such order amending the schedules of omnibus routes and services as he may think fit.

Another form of words that has been used is that a decision of the Minister on a question shall be final and conclusive, as in the case of the following sections of the Town Planning Act, 1925 (15 Geo. V. c. 16):

> "Section 1 (3). The expression 'land likely to be used for building purposes' shall include any land likely to be used as, or for the purpose of providing, open spaces, roads, streets, parks, pleasure or recreation grounds, or for the purpose of executing any work upon or under the land incidental to a town planning scheme, whether in the nature of a building work or not, and the decision of the Minister (of Health), whether land is likely to be used for building purposes or not, shall be final and conclusive."
>
> "Section 7 (3). If any question arises whether any building or work contravenes a town planning scheme, or whether any provision of a town planning scheme is not complied with in the erection or carrying out of any such building or work, that question shall be referred to the Minister (of Health), and shall, unless the parties otherwise agree, be determined by the Minister as arbitrator, and the decision of the Minister shall be final and conclusive."

There are other cases where it is expressly enacted that an order made by the Minister shall not be subject to an appeal to any Court. For instance, section 9 of the Roads Act, 1920 (10 & 11 Geo. V. c. 72), provides for the issuing by a county council to any manufacturer of or dealer in vehicles of a general licence in respect of all vehicles used by him, at a reduced duty, in lieu of separate licences in respect of each vehicle, and sub-section (3) is as follows:

> "If any person is aggrieved by the refusal of a council to issue a general licence under this section, he may appeal to the Minister (of Transport), and the Minister shall, on any such appeal, make such order in the matter as he thinks just, and the council shall comply with any order so made.
>
> "An order made by the Minister under this provision shall be final and not subject to appeal to any Court, and shall, on the application of the Minister, be enforceable by writ of mandamus."

A similar provision is contained in section 14 (3) of the same Act, as follows:

> "Where, upon application for a licence to ply for hire with an omnibus, the licensing authority either refuses to grant a licence or grants a licence subject to conditions, in either case the applicant shall have a right of appeal to the Minister of Transport from the decision of the licensing authority, and the Minister shall have power to make such order thereon as he thinks fit, and such order shall be binding on the licensing authority.
>
> "An order made by the Minister under this sub-section shall be final and not subject to appeal to any Court, and shall, on the application of the Minister, be enforceable by writ of mandamus."

The writ of mandamus here referred to is the prerogative writ issued from the King's Bench Division of the High Court, whereby the Court compels the performance of a duty of a public or quasi-public nature.

Sub-section (2) of section 4 of the London Traffic Act, 1924 (14 & 15 Geo. V. c. 34), provides, with reference to schemes for the closing of streets for works of road maintenance and improvement, that on the confirmation of any such scheme by the Minister of Transport, it shall become final and binding on all road authorities affected, and shall not be subject to appeal to any Court.

Another provision, which is frequently inserted, presumably because it is intended to deprive the Court of jurisdiction to inquire into the validity of a rule or order after it is once made, is that the rule or order shall take effect "as if enacted in this Act". This provision is apparently thought to give the rule or order the status of an Act of Parliament, the validity of which cannot, in any circumstances, be questioned.

So, for example, the Poor Law Act, 1927 (17 & 18 Geo. V. c. 14), which vests in the Minister of Health the direction and control of all matters relating to the administration of relief to the poor, provides by section 211:

> "(1) For executing the powers given to him by this Act the Minister shall make such rules and orders and regulations as he may think fit for—
>
> (*a*) the management of the poor;
>
> (*b*) the government of workhouses and the education of children therein;
>
> (*c*) the apprenticing of children of poor persons;
>
> (*d*) the guidance and control of boards of guardians and their officers as far as relates to the management or relief of the poor and subject to the provisions of this Act prescribing their duties;

(*e*) the making and entering into contracts in all matters relating to such management or relief, or to any expenditure for the relief of the poor;

(*f*) the keeping, examining, auditing, and allowing of accounts; and

(*g*) any purposes for which rules, orders, or regulations may be made under this Act and generally for the carrying of this Act into execution in all other respects.

"(2) All rules, orders, and regulations made by the Minister under this Act shall have effect as if enacted in this Act, subject, however, to the power of the Minister to suspend, alter, or rescind any such rule, order, or regulation."

The following are some other instances of this kind of provision, in order of date:

The Electricity Supply Act, 1919 (9 & 10 Geo. V. c. 100), section 34, provides—

"(1) The Board of Trade (now the Minister of Transport) and Electricity Commissioners may respectively make rules in relation to applications and other proceedings before them under this Act, and to the payments to be made in respect thereof, and to the publication of notices and advertisements and the manner in which and the time within which representations or objections with reference to any application or other proceedings are to be made, and to the holding of inquiries in such cases as they may think it advisable, and to the costs of such inquiries, and to any other matters arising in relation to their powers and duties under this Act.

"(2) Any rules made in pursuance of this section shall

be laid before Parliament as soon as may be *after they are made*, and shall have the same effect as if enacted in this Act."

Section 16 (1) & (2) of the Gas Regulation Act, 1920 (10 & 11 Geo. V. c. 28), is in practically the same terms as the foregoing section 34 of the Electricity Supply Act, 1919, omitting the reference to the Electricity Commissioners.

The Unemployment Insurance Act, 1920 (10 & 11 Geo. V. c. 30), provides, by section 35 (4), that any regulations made by the Minister of Labour under the Act shall have effect as if enacted in the Act.

The Housing Act, 1925 (15 Geo. V. c. 14), provides for the making of improvement and reconstruction schemes by local authorities, and the compulsory acquisition of property comprised in such schemes. The schemes require the confirmation by order of the Minister of Health, and by section 40 (5) it is provided that the order of the Minister when made shall have effect as if enacted in the Act.

Finally, in several recent statutes a provision is to be found which may be described as the "conclusive evidence provision",—a provision for which there would appear to be no possible justification.

The first three sub-sections of section 39 of the Small Holdings and Allotments Act, 1908 (8 Ed. VII. c. 36), which are a re-enactment of section 26 (1), (2), and (3) of the Small Holdings and Allotments Act of the previous year (7 Ed. VII. c. 54), are as follows:

"(1) Where a council (of a county, borough, urban district or parish) propose to purchase land compulsorily under this Act, the council may, subject to the provisions of Part I. of the First Schedule to this Act, submit to the Board (of Agriculture and Fisheries) an order, putting into force as respects the land specified in the order the provisions of the Lands Clauses Acts with respect to the purchase and taking of land otherwise than by agreement.

"(2) Where a council propose to hire land compulsorily, the council may submit to the Board an order for the compulsory hiring of the land specified in the order for a period not less than fourteen nor more than thirty-five years, and the provisions of Part I. of the First Schedule to this Act shall apply to the order in like manner as it applies to an order for compulsory purchase, with the substitution of 'hiring' for 'purchase' and with the modifications set out in Part II. of the Schedule.

"(3) An order under this section shall be of no force unless and until it is confirmed by the Board, and the Board may, subject to the provisions of the First Schedule to this Act, confirm the order either without modifications or subject to such modifications as they think fit, and an order when so confirmed shall become final and have effect as if enacted in this Act; *and the confirmation by the Board shall be conclusive evidence that the requirements of this Act have been complied with, and that the order has been duly made and is within the powers of this Act*."

Under the First Schedule to the Act the compensation to be paid for compulsory purchase is, in default of agreement, instead of being determined by arbitration in the usual way, to be determined by a single arbitrator appointed by the Board of Agriculture and Fisheries; and in the case of compulsory hiring, the amount of rent, in default of agreement, is to be determined by the valuation of a single valuer appointed by the Board.

In 1909 the effect of the above-cited sub-section 3 of section 39 was considered by a Divisional Court in the case of *Ex parte Ringer* (reported in 25 *Times Law Reports* at page 718). Mr. Ringer was a farmer, and, for the purpose of providing allotments an order had been made by the County Council, and confirmed by the Board of Agriculture and Fisheries, empowering the County Council to purchase compulsorily one of his farms which he wished to retain as being necessary for the profitable working of his other farms. An application was made to the Court for a rule *nisi* for a writ of certiorari to bring up the order to be quashed, on the ground that it was clear that the Board had not given effect to the restriction contained in section 41 (2) of the Act, which is as follows:

> "A council in making, and the Board in confirming, an order for the compulsory acquisition of land shall have regard to the extent of land held or occupied in the locality by any owner or tenant, and to the convenience of other property belonging to or occupied by the same owner or tenant, and shall, so far as practicable, avoid taking an undue or inconvenient quantity of land from any one owner or tenant, and for that purpose where part only of a holding is taken shall take into consideration the size and character of the existing agricultural buildings not proposed to be taken which were used in connection with the holding and the quantity and nature of the land available for occupation therewith."

In delivering judgement dismissing the application, Mr. Justice Darling, as he then was, said

> "the section gave to an order made by a public department the absolute finality and effect of an Act of Parliament. . . . Here there was a public department put in a position of absolute supremacy . . . and they could only say that Parliament had enacted only last year that the Board of Agriculture in acting as they did should be no more impeachable than Parliament itself."

Mr. Justice Jelf said that the case presented an illustration of the length to which Parliament had the right to go in ousting the powers and jurisdiction of Courts of Law. If a majority in Parliament were successful in passing an Act of Parliament which had that effect,

> "then the jurisdiction of the Courts of Law, in matters in which some people might think it was desirable that even Government departments should be under control of the Courts, was nevertheless ousted, and the Court had no power to interfere with the decision of the department."

Now is it, or is it not, tolerably certain that the majority in Parliament were not aware of any such provision in the Bill when they passed it, and that very few of those who were aware of it had any knowledge of its effect? To provide that the confirmation of an order by the Board should be conclusive evidence that the requirements of the Act had been complied with, and that the order had been duly made and was within the powers of the Act, was a direct encouragement to the Board to disregard the requirements of the Act, and to exceed the powers intended by the Legislature to be conferred on them. In passing such a clause Parliament, it may be thought, was really stultifying itself, because, having inserted express provisions in the Act for the protection of persons liable to have their property taken without their consent, and having enacted that the council in making, and the Board in confirming, an order must have regard to those provisions, it then, by means of this "conclusive evidence clause" rendered such provisions nugatory, and, so far as victims are concerned, a mockery.

Notwithstanding these criticisms from the Bench, similar clauses have since been inserted in various other statutes dealing with compulsory purchase and compulsory hiring of land.

The Housing, Town Planning, etc., Act, 1909 (9 Ed. VII. c. 44), in the First Schedule contains provisions as to the compulsory acquisition of land by a local authority for the purposes of Part III. of the Housing of the Working Classes Act, 1890, which deals with the provision of working-class lodging-houses, and clause (2) of the Schedule is as follows:

> "An order under this Schedule shall be of no force unless and until it is confirmed by the (Local Government) Board, and the Board may confirm the order either without modification or subject to such modifications as they may think fit, and an order so confirmed shall, save as otherwise expressly provided by this Schedule, become final and have effect as if enacted in this Act: *and the confirmation shall be conclusive evidence*

that the requirements of this Act have been complied with, and that the order has been duly made and is within the powers of this Act."

The provisions of the First Schedule to the last-mentioned Act are applied by the Education Act, 1918 (8 & 9 Geo. V. c. 39), section 34 (1), to the compulsory acquisition of land by local education authorities for the purpose of any of their powers or duties under the Education Acts, with the substitution of the Board of Education for the Local Government Board.

Section 16 of the Salmon and Freshwater Fisheries Act, 1923 (13 & 14 Geo. V. c. 16), provides for the compulsory purchase or hiring of obstructions and fisheries by Fishery Boards by order, confirmed by the Minister of Agriculture and Fisheries, and sub-section (5) of the section is in the same terms as clause (2) of the First Schedule to the Housing, Town Planning, etc., Act, 1909 (above), with the substitution of "Minister" for "Board".

So, too, the Housing Act, 1925 (15 Geo. V. c. 14), which provides for compulsory purchase of land by local authorities by means of an order confirmed by the Minister of Health in accordance with the Third Schedule, for the purpose of providing houses for the working classes, contains a clause (clause (2)) in the Third Schedule which is in practically the same terms as clause (2) of the First Schedule of the Act of 1909.

Under section 10 of the London Traffic Act, 1924 (14 & 15 Geo. V. c. 34), the Minister of Transport has power to make regulations to have effect in the London Traffic Area for relieving and facilitating traffic in and near

London. Such regulations may provide for the suspension or modification of any Acts of Parliament, bye-laws, or regulations dealing with the same subject-matter as the regulations made by the Minister, or of any Acts conferring power of making bye-laws or regulations dealing with the same subject-matter. Sub-section (3) of the section provides that:

> "Any such regulations may provide for imposing fines recoverable summarily in respect of breaches thereof not exceeding in the case of a first offence twenty pounds, or in case of a second or subsequent offence fifty pounds, together with, in the case of a continuing offence, a further fine not exceeding five pounds for each day the offence continues after notice of the offence has been given in such manner as may be prescribed by the regulations."

And by sub-section (6):

> "*The making of any regulations under this section shall be conclusive evidence that the requirements of this section have been complied with.*"

The excuses which are offered even by the most able of the apologists of the new despotism are sometimes rather entertaining. It is said that Parliament simply has not time to do otherwise than delegate legislative power; that Parliament, even if it had the time, has not the requisite aptitude for the work; and that, after all, it is not the task of Parliament, but the task of the Executive, to govern the country. The last of these three propositions is said to constitute the "greatest justification for delegated legislation". Now, to some onlookers it may occur that if this threefold defence is really to be regarded as a fair and considered statement of the frame of mind which exhibits itself in the new despotism, nothing could well be more grave. For what does it mean? Let it be granted, for the sake of the argument, that there are matters of detail which can hardly be debated at length across the floor of the House of Commons. Let it be granted, again, for the sake of the argument, that from time to time an Act of Parliament may involve technical matters which require careful and protracted consideration at the hands of experts and specialists. Neither of these circumstances, nor the pair of them in combination, can be said to afford the smallest reason why the work which is done should be done behind the back of Parliament, or without its knowledge and real assent. Nor do these or any other circumstances afford a reason why the order which is made, or the decision which is given, should be so contrived as to be beyond review in a Court of Law. As for the third of the propositions, if it contemplates anything over and above what in a particular emergency may be rendered necessary by "sudden causes and occasions" or "promptitude to meet the exigency of the case", it is not easy to imagine anything more mischievous or more subversive. True, it is indeed the task of the Executive to govern the country. But it is the task of Parliament to make the laws, and the real business of the Executive is to govern the country in accordance with the laws which Parliament has made. Is it not precisely because it is the task of the Executive to govern the country that it is so dangerous to hand over to the Executive the power of making laws as well, and of making them in ways which, while a kind of formal homage is paid to the Sovereignty of Parliament, have the effect of employing the Sovereignty of Parliament to oust the jurisdiction of the Courts?

Those who defend the system of departmental decision, without reasons given, without the possibility of appeal, and behind the back of the other party, are heard from time to time to say that it is cheap. Yet it may be much too dear at the price. They deplore the costliness of litigation. What they mean is that they do not wish the Courts to stand between the departments and the taxpayer. *Sunt lacrimae rerum*—also *crocodilorum*. Things have their tears, and crocodiles have theirs. Litigation is not necessarily costly. Of course if everybody at the same time insists on briefing one or other of a very small group of fashionable counsel, those favoured persons naturally, in order to protect themselves, increase their fees. Otherwise the burden of their work would be greater than they could bear. But there is no lack of ability at the Bar, and there are scores of highly competent barristers whose fees are not in any degree exorbitant. Besides, it must occur to anybody whose opinion is not fixed beforehand that the argument based on the cost of litigation, even if it were sincere, would necessarily go much too far. If the taxpayer is not to be allowed to appeal from a departmental decision because the appeal might prove expensive for him, in what cases, if any, is an appeal to be desired? Nor is it necessary to elaborate the point that the excellence of a statutory right of appeal consists, not in multiplying appeals, but in encouraging decisions of such a kind that appeals against them will not seem attractive.

The gist of the matter was forcibly and concisely expressed by Sir John Marriott in his article on "Law and Liberty" in the *Fortnightly Review* for July 1928.

> "It is my profound conviction", he wrote, "that the prevailing and increasing disposition on the part of the British Parliament to confer upon the Executive quasi-judicial and quasi-legislative functions is wholly mischievous and ought to be resisted. 'The power of the Crown has increased, is increasing, and ought to be diminished.' So ran Dunning's famous resolution. Most of us would be startled if such a resolution were carried or even proposed in the House of Commons to-day. Yet if for 'Crown' we substitute 'Executive', there is at least as much ground for proposing that resolution to-day as there was in the third decade of the reign of George III."

Closely connected with the subject-matter of the present inquiry is the mischief arising from the obscurity of the language of so many statutes. To make a statute unintelligible is not the same thing as to make a departmental decision final, but either course may defeat the taxpayer. The obscurity of the language of statutes is matter for a separate treatise. It is due sometimes to ill-considered amendments, sometimes to the ambiguous use of terms, sometimes to a passion for "simplifying" the law by reiterating old expressions with new meanings. But above all it is due to legislation by reference, and to the fixed and settled determination not to set out the matter clearly and completely. It is not many months ago since the Revenue

Judge expressed himself pretty plainly in Court upon the scandal of introducing Bills, or enacting statutes, in the complicated and unintelligible form of many of the statutes referred to in the particular case. If he was bewildered as an expert in that very branch of the law, what must be the position of the ordinary taxpayer? The answer given by the Law Officer who was conducting the case for the Crown was illuminating. He said that it would not be possible to get the Bills through the House of Commons in any other form. Now, this answer was not Machiavellian nor probably was it intended to be facetious. It seems to have been intended rather as a bald statement of literal fact. In other words, the meaning appears to be that, if Bills which impose or regulate taxes are to be got through the House of Commons within reasonable time, care must be taken that they shall not expose too large a surface for possible attack. Or, to put the matter more shortly, to be intelligible is to be found out, and to be found out is to be defeated. If this doctrine be true, it may be thought to throw an interesting light upon representative institutions and self-government, as in some quarters understood. Is it conceivable that a Parliament may some day arise which will refuse to pass lumps of undigested legislation, and will enact only that which it understands and definitely intends? If the output of legislation were in consequence smaller, it might not be a calamity.

CHAPTER VI

DEPARTMENTAL LEGISLATION

There are two kinds of delegated legislation, one based on the prerogative of the Crown, and the other deriving its force from some Act of Parliament expressly giving power to legislate with regard to a particular matter either to the King in Council or to a public minister or department or some other authority. The term "prerogative" comprises such powers as are exerciseable by the executive Government without express authority from Parliament. There are many matters which were formerly the subject of prerogative legislation exclusively, but which are now dealt with by Act of Parliament, and it is a principle of the Constitution that, when Parliament has given express power to legislate in reference to a particular matter, and has provided by whom and subject to what limitations the power shall be exercised, the prerogative power of legislation in regard to that matter is superseded. At the present day prerogative legislation is chiefly concerned with the Army and the Navy, the Civil and Diplomatic Services, and the government of Crown Colonies, Dependencies, and the Channel Islands. All prerogative legislation is in theory subject to review by the Courts of Law, and may be treated as void if found to be *ultra vires*.

The largest and most important part of the statutory

delegated legislation is comprised in what are known as "Statutory Rules and Orders". All of this legislation derives its force from the Act of Parliament by which the legislative power is given, and not from the authority by whom the power was exercised. Consequently, in order to ascertain whether a particular statutory rule or order is *intra vires* or *ultra vires*, it is necessary to look at the terms of the authorizing statute to see whether the legislating authority has acted within the limits of its mandate, and, to speak generally, the validity of much statutory delegated legislation may be judicially challenged, and, if any such legislation is held to be invalid, it may be treated as void or quashed. Expedients have, however, in many cases been resorted to for the purpose of ousting this power of judicial review and rendering statutory rules and orders unchallengeable as Acts of Parliament themselves; and, of course, no Court can question the validity of an Act of Parliament. These expedients are referred to elsewhere.

Save that their validity can in many cases be judicially questioned, statutory rules, regulations, and orders are as much part of the law, and as effective, as Acts of Parliament, and, in the matter of quantity, this kind of delegated legislation has in recent years enormously exceeded the amount of direct legislation by statute. Nor is such delegated legislation by any means confined to matters of detail or of small importance. Very wide and general powers are sometimes given to a public department to make regulations "for the purpose of carrying this Act into effect", and the Act itself may merely state the subjects in regard to which the regulations may be made without any further indication of the kind of legislation intended to be authorized, this crucial matter being left entirely to the discretion of the department. Sometimes power is given to the rule-making authority to revoke or alter express provisions of the statute under which the regulations are made in regard to matters of prime importance.

It is provided by section 32 (3) of the Interpretation Act, 1889, that where an Act passed after the commencement of that Act "confers a power to make any rules, regulations, or by-laws, the power shall, unless the contrary intention appears, be construed as including a power, exerciseable in the like manner and subject to the like consent and conditions, if any, to rescind, revoke, amend, or vary the rules, regulations, or by-laws". It would appear, however, that this provision does not apply to statutory orders, as distinguished from rules, regulations, and by-laws, and therefore, unless a power of revocation or amendment is expressly conferred, an order of a legislative character cannot be revoked or varied by the authority by whom it was made.

It is tolerably obvious that the system of delegation by Parliament of powers of legislation is within certain limits necessary, at least as regards matters of detail, because it is impossible, if only for want of time, for Parliament to deal adequately and in detail with all the matters calling, or supposed to call, for legislation. Indeed, without a drastic alteration of its methods of procedure, it would be impossible for Parliament to deal adequately with even a comparatively small part of the present-day volume of departmental legislation. It may also be conceded that the system, if not abused, and subject to proper safeguards, may have its uses. It is the abuse of the system that calls for criticism, and perhaps the greatest abuse, and the one most likely to lead to arbitrary and unreasonable legislation, is the ousting of the jurisdiction of the Courts.

A valuable security against hasty and unreasonable legislation is a provision, which is sometimes inserted in statutes giving legislative powers, requiring that, before the powers are actually exercised, persons interested shall be notified and given the opportunity to make objections or suggestions, and in some cases requiring a public inquiry to be held. Section 1 of the Rules Publication Act, 1893 (56 & 57 Vict. c. 66), provides as follows:

> "1. (1) At least forty days before making any statutory rules to which this section applies, notice of the proposal to make the rules, and of the place where copies of the draft rules may be obtained, shall be published in the *London Gazette*.
>
> "(2) During those forty days any public body may obtain copies of such draft rules on payment of not exceeding three pence per folio, and any representations or suggestions made in writing by a public body interested to the authority proposing to make the rules shall be taken into consideration by that authority before finally settling the rules; and on the expiration of those forty days the rules may be made by the rule-making authority, either as originally drawn or as amended by such authority, and shall come into operation forthwith or at such time as may be prescribed in the rules.
>
> "(3) Any enactment which provides that any statutory

rules to which this section applies shall not come into operation for a specified period after they are made is hereby repealed, but this repeal shall not affect section thirty-seven of the Interpretation Act, 1889.

"(4) The statutory rules to which this section applies are those made in pursuance of any Act of Parliament which directs the statutory rules to be laid before Parliament, but do not include any statutory rules if the same or a draft thereof are required to be laid before Parliament for any period before the rules come into operation, nor do they include rules made by the Local Government Board for England or Ireland, the Board of Trade, or the Revenue Departments, or by or for the purposes of the Post Office; nor rules made by the Board of Agriculture under the Contagious Diseases (Animals) Act, 1878, and the Acts amending the same.

"(5) This section shall not apply to Scotland.

"(6) In the case of any rules which it is proposed shall extend to Ireland, publication in the *Dublin Gazette* of the notice required by this section shall be requisite in addition to, or, if they extend to Ireland only, in lieu of, publication in the *London Gazette*."

Section 37 of the Interpretation Act, 1889, referred to above in sub-section (3), provides that where an Act passed after the commencement of that Act

"is not to come into operation immediately on the passing thereof, and confers powers to make any appointment, to make, grant, or issue any instrument, that is to say, any Order in Council, order, warrant, scheme, letters patent, rules, regulations, or by-laws, to give notices, to prescribe forms, or to do any other thing for the purposes of the Act, that power may, unless the con-

> trary intention appears, be exercised at any time after the passing of the Act, so far as may be necessary or expedient for the purpose of bringing the Act into operation at the date of the commencement thereof, subject to this restriction, that any instrument made under the power shall not, unless the contrary intention appears in the Act, or the contrary is necessary for bringing the Act into operation, come into operation until the Act comes into operation."

It will at once be observed that the foregoing provisions of the Rules Publication Act have a very limited operation.

First, they apply only to statutory rules made in pursuance of an Act which directs that they are to be laid before Parliament, and it is only in a comparatively small number of the statutes giving power to make statutory rules that there is any such direction.

Secondly, it is doubtful whether the provisions apply to statutory orders, as distinguished from statutory rules, regulations, and by-laws. Probably they do not. (See the definition of "statutory rules" for the purposes of the Act below.)

Thirdly, the provisions do not apply if the rules or a draft thereof are required to be laid before Parliament for any period before the rules come into operation.

Fourthly, the provisions do not apply at all to rules made by the Local Government Board (now the Ministry of Health), the Board of Trade, or the Revenue Departments, or by or for the purposes of the Post Office, nor to rules made by the Ministry of Agriculture and Fisheries under the Contagious Diseases (Animals) Acts.

Fifthly, the provisions of the section have been expressly excluded by various Acts conferring rule-making powers.

Lastly, even when the section does apply, its provisions may always be evaded by a certificate of urgency, section 2 of the Act providing that

> "where a rule-making authority certifies that on account of urgency or any special reason any rule should come into immediate operation, it shall be lawful for such authority to make any such rules to come into operation forthwith as provisional rules, but such provisional rules shall only continue in force until rules have been made in accordance with the foregoing provisions of this Act."

It is to be noted that provisional rules not only come into operation forthwith, but continue in force until rules have been duly made in accordance with the provisions of section 1. If, therefore, rules are never made in accordance with those provisions, and there is no obligation to make rules in accordance with them, the provisional rules will remain in force indefinitely, and provisional rules are as valid and effective in every respect as if the provisions of section 1 of the Act had been complied with.

A provision which is sometimes found in statutes giving power to make regulations is to the effect that the regulations shall be laid before each House of Parliament as soon as may be after they are made, and that if an address is presented to His Majesty by either House within a certain number of days (usually twenty or thirty days), on which that House has sat, next after any such regulation is laid before it, praying that the regulation may be annulled, His

Majesty in Council may annul the regulation, and it shall thenceforth be void, but without prejudice to the validity of anything previously done thereunder. In such a case the regulations take effect as soon as they are made, and the provisions of section 1 of the Rules Publication Act therefore apply, unless they are expressly excluded or the regulations are made by one of the excepted departments. Regulations are very rarely annulled in pursuance of such a provision, but this fact does not necessarily mean that they are unobjectionable. It may be that they escape because no member of Parliament has taken the trouble to weigh and consider them. The liability to annulment may, however, have the effect of making the legislating department somewhat more careful than it would otherwise be.

The following are examples of other types of provisions to be found in statutes of the kind under consideration:—

(*a*) Before the order comes into force it shall be laid before each House of Parliament for a period of not less than thirty days during which that House is sitting, and, if either of those Houses before the expiration of those thirty days presents an address to His Majesty against the order or any part thereof, no further proceedings shall be taken thereon, without prejudice to the making of any new order. Here the order does not come into operation until the expiration of the thirty days, and the provisions of section 1 of the Rules Publication Act have no application.

(*b*) The order shall be laid, as soon as may be after it is made, before each House of Parliament, but shall not come into operation unless and until it has been approved, either with or without modification, by a resolution passed by each such House. When there is this provision, the order is in the nature of a proposal, which has no effect until it has been approved by resolution of both Houses. It is nevertheless delegated legislation, because a resolution of both Houses is not equivalent to an Act of Parliament, and, in the absence of provision to the contrary, the order, notwithstanding a resolution of approval, may be open to judicial challenge on the score of *ultra vires*.

Until 1890 there was no regular publication of statutory rules and orders, and often the only means of finding them was by a search through the *London Gazette*. Since that year they have been printed and published on a systematic plan and placed on sale. There are annual volumes, published by authority, containing every statutory rule and order (other than those of a local, personal, or temporary character) issued during the year, and also containing classified lists of the local orders of the year, and tables showing the temporary orders which have come into force and expired during the year, and the effect of the year's rules and orders on statutes and on the statutory rules and orders previously in force. There is also an edition in thirteen volumes, issued in 1904, of "The Statutory Rules and Orders Revised", which contains all the statutory rules and orders (other than those of a local, personal, or temporary character) which were in force on the 31st December 1903.

The official printing and sale of statutory rules and orders are now regulated by the provisions of section 3 of the Rules Publication Act, 1893, and the Regulations, dated the 9th August 1894, made thereunder. Section 3 of the Act is as follows:

"3. (1) All statutory rules made after the thirty-first day of December next after the passing of this Act shall forthwith after they are made be sent to the Queen's printer of Acts of Parliament, and shall, in accordance with regulations made by the Treasury, with the concurrence of the Lord Chancellor and the Speaker of the House of Commons, be numbered, and (save as provided by the regulations) printed, and sold by him.

"(2) Any statutory rules may, without prejudice to any other mode of citation, be cited by the number so given as above mentioned and the calendar year.

"(3) Where any statutory rules are required by any Act to be published or notified in the London, Edinburgh, or Dublin *Gazette*, a notice in the *Gazette* of the rules having been made, and of the place where copies of them can be purchased, shall be sufficient compliance with the said requirement.

"(4) Regulations under this section may provide for the different treatment of statutory rules which are of the nature of public Acts, and of those which are of the nature of local and personal or private Acts; and may determine the classes of cases in which the exercise of a statutory power by any rule-making authority constitutes or does not constitute the making of a statutory rule within the meaning of this section, and may provide for the exemption from this section of any such classes.

"(5) In the making of such regulations, each Government department concerned shall be consulted, and due regard had to the views of that department."

Section 4 of the Act defines "statutory rules" as meaning

"rules, regulations, or by-laws made under any Act of Parliament which (*a*) relate to any Court in the United Kingdom, or to the procedure, practice, costs, or fees therein, or to any fees or matters applying generally throughout England, Scotland, or Ireland; or (*b*) are made by Her Majesty in Council, the Judicial Committee, the Treasury, the Lord Chancellor of Great Britain, or the Lord Lieutenant or the Lord Chancellor of Ireland, or a Secretary of State, the Admiralty, the Board of Trade, the Local Government Board for England or Ireland, the Chief Secretary for Ireland, or any other Government Department":

and "rule-making authority" as including "every authority authorized to make any statutory rules".

The Regulations made in pursuance of section 3 of the Act provide that every exercise of a statutory power by a rule-making authority which is of a legislative and not an executive character shall be held to be a statutory rule within that section; but an exercise of a statutory power which is confirmed only by a rule-making authority shall not be held to be a statutory rule within the section. It would, therefore, seem that, unlike section 1, section 3 applies to statutory orders as well as rules, regulations, or by-laws, provided that they are made, and not merely confirmed, by one of the authorities indicated in section 4 of the Act. But, apparently, only orders which are made directly under an Act of Parliament by a rule-making authority are considered statutory orders. If a rule or order made in pursuance of an Act of Parliament provides, by way of sub-delegation, for the making of further orders, these further orders are not themselves regarded as "made under any Act of Parliament", and are therefore altogether outside the scope of the Rules Publication Act.

The Regulations further provide that a distinction shall be drawn between statutory rules which are general and those which are local and personal, and that the distinction shall follow, unless in exceptional circumstances, that which is adopted between public Acts and local and personal Acts of Parliament. Statutory rules similar to public general Acts are to be printed *in extenso* in a classified form in the annual volume, and the volume is to have merely a list of the statutory rules which are similar to local and personal Acts. To speak broadly, a Public Act may be described as one which concerns the community as a whole, a local Act is one the effect of which is confined to a particular district or locality, and a personal Act is one for the benefit of a particular person or particular persons, such as a Naturalization or Divorce Act. Temporary rules, which have ceased to be in force at the time of the publication of the annual volume, or will so cease a short time afterwards, are not to be included in the volume unless the rule-making authority desire them to be included.

The Treasury, with the concurrence of the Lord Chancellor and the Speaker of the House of Commons, may direct the exclusion from publication at length in any annual volume, of any rules which it seems to them unnecessary so to publish by reason of their annual or other periodical renewal; and may exempt from section 3 of the Act and from the Regulations any statutory rule or class of statutory rules which may be determined by them to be confidential.

The apologists and champions of the new despotism exhibit, indeed, remarkable gifts of inaccuracy. One such writer, in a volume recently published, permitted himself to say generally of statutory delegated legislation:

> "There is no theoretical limit to which this delegation may be carried, and it has been carried very far in recent years. *Usually* Parliament retains some control by the inclusion in the Act of a provision that the rules drawn up by the executive, in exercise of a power so bestowed upon them by the legislature, shall be laid before Parliament, in draft, for a certain number of days before becoming operative, and will become operative only in the absence of an address from either House against the draft or any part thereof."

This passage is, of course, extremely misleading. Such a provision as that which is here described as usual is in fact very rare. It is probably not to be found in as many as one per cent of the statutes conferring legislative powers, and in the great majority of such statutes there is no provision for parliamentary control of any sort. In another passage the public is assured that

> "Parliament . . . has also bestowed on Ministers very wide powers to make Rules and Orders covering a multitude of subjects. . . . Generally speaking . . . they have *normally* to be submitted to Parliament, either as an essential pre-requisite to their validity or as a precautionary measure after they have come into force."

Here, again, the use of the word "normally" is calculated to give an entirely false impression. The simple truth is, of course, that much the larger number of statutory rules and orders are not required to be submitted to Parliament at all.

Elsewhere inaccuracy takes a different turn. The reader is told that:

> "In the first place the very wideness of the language which is used in the Statute delegating legislation to an administrative body may in effect oust the jurisdiction of the Court. This was so in the powers given by section 1 (1) of the Defence of the Realm Consolidation Act, 1914."

This statement manifestly involves a misreading of the effect of the decision in *R.* v. *Halliday*, to which reference is made. In that case it was held that the Regulation which was in question was not *ultra vires*, but the jurisdiction of the Court to review the regulation and decide whether it was *intra* or *ultra vires* was fully recognized. And in *Chester* v. *Bateson* (1920), 1 K.B. 829, another Regulation made under the same statute was held to be *ultra vires*. Similarly, it is a little surprising to read that:

> "Where the Order cannot be made unless both Houses by resolution approve the draft, an appeal to the Courts against an Order so made would *obviously* be in the nature of an attempted interference with parliamentary functions. Nor would such an appeal be any more effective where an Order is laid before both Houses for 21 or 28 days, and can during that period be annulled by a resolution of either House. Negatively, Parliament has approved it. From the point of view of appeal on the ground of *ultra vires*, therefore, the only class of delegation which gives an appellant a sporting chance is that

in which the language of the Statute is reasonably restricted in scope and where submission to Parliament is not required."

The first sentence in this passage ignores the dicta of Younger, L.J. (as he then was), in *R.* v. *Electricity Commissioners* (1924), 1 K.B., at p. 212, and the word "obviously" is therefore not justified, even though it be assumed that the Court has no jurisdiction in such a case to quash the Order as *ultra vires*. As for the rest of the passage, there is certainly no authority in support of the views expressed, and they appear to be entirely erroneous. In yet another passage it is asserted that

> "the next administrative safeguard is that of public notice of intention to exercise legislative powers. Here the provisions of section 1 of the Rules Publication Act, 1893 (56 & 57 Vict. c. 66), have wide application. . . . These provisions give ample opportunity for criticism before the rules are made. . . ."

In this passage, as is plain, there is no hint of the extremely limited scope of these provisions, or of section 2 of the Act, which makes evasion so absurdly easy. The "ample opportunity for criticism" exists with regard to comparatively few statutory rules, and in the case of statutory orders does not exist at all.

But the variety of inaccuracy is not yet exhausted. In the same volume the writer asserts that:

> "In contract, whether the private individual proceeds by way of petition of right, or whether he brings into court directly one of those heads of departments of the

> Crown who have been made more accessible to actions, by statutory provision that they may sue or be sued, he will be met by the array of the Crown's prerogatives in pleading and procedure, viz. those as to Discovery, Interrogatories, Costs, and the Statute of Limitations, and so on, which place him at a serious disadvantage."

Here again the pedestrian fact is that, in such proceedings as those which are referred to, costs are payable as if there were an action between subject and subject, the prerogative of the Crown in this respect having been abolished. The Statute of Limitations cannot be pleaded by the Crown in answer to a Petition of Right. But this circumstance is obviously to the advantage of the suppliant. It certainly cannot operate to his disadvantage. With regard to discovery, the plaintiff or suppliant is no doubt at some disadvantage. But even in that respect the disadvantage is, in practice, more imaginary than real. It is not easy to know what is meant by "and so on". But it is in respect of discovery alone that, in such proceedings as are in question, the party suing can be said to be at any sort of disadvantage. Nor, to be fair, is there any real foundation for the statement which follows, that "It has long been difficult to bring a successful action against either a Government department, or even an official, for any dereliction of duty", where such dereliction of duty has caused loss or injury to a private individual. As to the practice, referred to in the same context, whereby the Government pays damages awarded against a public official for a wrong done in the course of his service, this, again, is obviously to the advantage of the injured party, because he has the certainty, if he is successful, of recovering his damages and costs.

Finally, the author, while he says that "it is important that effective safeguards should be imposed upon all administrative legislation", repeats in stronger language one of his misleading statements already mentioned, as follows:

> "*The large majority* of Statutes delegating legislative powers merely require that the resulting Order shall be laid before Parliament as soon as may be after it has been made; or add that such an Order shall be annulled if either House pass a resolution to that effect within twenty-one or twenty-eight days from the date when the Order is first brought before Parliament."

The passage, if it is to be made accurate, must be amended so as to read:

> "*A small minority* of Statutes delegating legislative powers require that the resulting rule or order shall be laid before Parliament as soon as may be after it has been made; and *in rare cases* add that such a rule or order shall be annulled if either House, etc."

From these and the like statements two facts seem clearly to emerge. One is that there is in existence a body of persons who, for some reason or other, are extremely anxious to put the best face upon the encroachments of bureaucracy. The other is that, in the way in which they perform their task, accuracy is not their strong point.

Referring to instances in which the statute has been so framed as to provide that rules and orders made under it shall have the same effect as if enacted in the Act, Mr. C. K. Allen (now Professor of Jurisprudence in the University of Oxford) wrote in his well-known work on "Law in the Making", published in 1927, that this form of delegation

> "is more than delegation—it makes the executive not merely a deputy but a plenipotentiary. And it becomes increasingly common. The result can only be confusion in the working of the constitution and obscurity in the legal conception of the Sovereignty of the State. While we have never accepted in full the French doctrine of the separation of powers, it is clear that unless there is some intelligible and consistent demarcation between the different spheres of public law, antagonisms and inconsequences must ensue. It is incompatible with the whole theory of our constitution that the executive and judicial functions should seriously overlap, but there can be little doubt that the present tendency is not only to invest the executive with judicial powers, but to oust the control of the regular Courts and make the executive judge in its own cause."

Nobody is likely to deny that the necessities and emergencies of the Great War afforded a signal opportunity for departmental legislation and produced an enormous expansion in the annual output of rules, orders, and regulations. But the encroachments of bureaucracy had begun well before the war, and assuredly they have survived it. During the year 1920, for example, the total output only of those sets of rules and orders which are officially registered was no less than 2473. The corresponding figure for the year 1927 was 1349. Does any human being read through this mass of departmental legislation? Is any human brain supposed to have mastered and to retain its contents? During the year 1927 Parliament passed forty-three Public General Acts, and it has been pointed out that twenty-six out of those forty-three Acts contemplate or authorize the making of Orders in Council, rules, or regulations. Now, no doubt the common phrase "everybody is supposed to know the law" is not quite accurate. Mr. Justice Maule put the matter, as was to be expected, with perfect accuracy when he said in *Martindale* v. *Falkner* (2 C.B. p. 719):

> "There is no presumption in this country that every person knows the law. It would be contrary to common sense and reason if it were so. The rule is that ignorance of the law shall not excuse a man or relieve him from the consequences of crime or from liability upon a contract."

If the citizen is permitted to be ignorant, his ignorance is not permitted to be an excuse. Meantime the mass of subsidiary, departmental, or delegated legislation (these are different names for the same thing) is manufactured to an extent which passes understanding. The citizen does not know what it is. He does not know where to find it He probably would not understand it, and its relation to the rest of the law, if he did find it. But he is bound by it all the same.

> "Everywhere in our statute-book", as Mr. Cecil T. Carr writes, in his extremely valuable lectures on "Delegated Legislation", "the same process is visible. The action of our Acts of Parliament grows more and more

> dependent upon subsidiary legislation. More than half our modern Acts are to this extent incomplete statements of law. If anyone opens at random a recent annual volume of public general statutes, he will not have to turn many pages before finding a provision that His Majesty may make Orders in Council, or that some public body or officer or department may make rules or regulations, contributing some addition to the substance or the detail or the working of that particular Act."

The paradox is that it is precisely in the labyrinth of departmental legislation that the citizen, if time permitted, might find the particular order or prohibition which should direct his conduct, and which, if it be ignored, is ignored at his peril. As a rule he is not interested in what may be termed the immensities and eternities of legislation or of jurisprudence. But he is, or may be, profoundly interested in the rules or orders subsidiary to a statute, for the very reason that they deal with particulars, and the particular is the thing to be done.

It may be hoped that Sir Lynden Macassey, K.C., is right in saying, in his valuable article upon "Law-making by Government Departments" (*Journal of Comparative Legislation and International Law*, vol. 5, part 1, p. 73), that the flood of restrictions and regulations with the force of law that overspread the country during the war opened the eyes of the public to the extent to which liberty may be imperilled by such a system.

> "No safeguard", he says, "can possibly provide against the chief inherent objection. Government bills are forced

through Parliament under the pressure of the Government Whips; there is little time for discussion of their provisions either in the House or in Committee; legislation is passed in the most general terms and left to some Government department to apply as it thinks fit under machinery or rules to be made by it; the Cabinet is therefore in a position through its member at the head of a Government department to embark on a particular policy which has never in any detail been discussed in Parliament or communicated to the public. If the action of the department is challenged in the House, the Government can say, as has been done, that the action of the department is fully within the powers conferred upon it by the Legislature. Not merely in Great Britain, but in the Dominions, there is a rising feeling of hostility to legislation by Government departments, except in cases plainly necessary."

An interesting example—interesting both in itself and as a specimen of method—may be found under the Public Health Amendment Act, 1907. By section 3 (1) of that Act the Local Government Board (now the Ministry of Health) may, on the application of a Local Authority, by Order declare any part or section of that Act to be in force in the district of that Local Authority, and may declare any enactments in any local Act, which appear to the Ministry to contain provisions similar to or inconsistent with any such part or section, to be no longer in force in that district. By section 3 (3) any such Order may declare any part or any section to be in force *subject to such necessary adaptations as are specified in the Order*. Section 30, which is in Part II. of the Act, reads as follows:

"30. With respect to the repairing or enclosing of dangerous places the following provisions shall have effect (namely):

"(1) If in any situation fronting, adjoining, or abutting on any street or public footpath, any building, wall, fence, steps, structure, or other thing, or any well, excavation, reservoir, pond, stream, dam, or bank is, for want of sufficient repair, protection, or enclosure dangerous to the persons lawfully using the street or footpath, the local authority may, by notice in writing served upon the owner, require him, within the period specified in the notice and hereinafter in this section referred to as the 'prescribed period', to repair, remove, protect, or enclose the same so as to prevent any danger therefrom:

"(2) If, after service of the notice on the owner, he shall neglect to comply with the requirements thereof within the prescribed period, the local authority may cause such works as they think proper to be done for effecting such repair, removal, protection, or enclosure, and the expenses thereof shall be payable by the owner, and may be recovered summarily as a civil debt."

Under these provisions an Order was made on the 11th August 1911, relating to the City of Durham and Framwellgate, by which the Local Government Board declared (*inter alia*) Part II. to be in force in the district as if the following words were added to section 30, namely:

"Nothing in this Section shall apply to any wall or other structure in so far as the same is used either for the support of any street or public footpath, or for the protection of any street or public footpath from damage or obstruction, by reason of the surface of the street or footpath being above or below the level of the surface of the adjoining land *unless* the wall or other structure was built after the street or footpath became a highway repairable by the inhabitants at large by or at the expense of a person other than the highway authority responsible for the repair of the street or footpath."

The effect is to enact important provisions with regard to the liability to repair retaining walls (sometimes 10 to 30 feet high) which support roadways, and to alter the law by an enactment which Parliament has never seen or considered.

CHAPTER VII

THE INDEPENDENCE OF THE JUDICIARY

Every student of history knows that many of the most significant victories for freedom and justice have been won in the English Law Courts, and that the liberties of Englishmen are closely bound up with the complete independence of the judges. When, for any reason or combination of reasons, it has happened that there has been lack of courage on the Judicial Bench, the enemies of equality before the law have succeeded, and the administration of the law has been brought into disrepute. In particular there have been, in the long course of English history, periods and occasions when the Executive has endeavoured, not entirely without success, to control and to pervert the course of judicial decision. It was not without good reason that, in 1701, those who were responsible for the Act of Settlement were careful to provide that judges could not be removed except on the address of both Houses of Parliament. For more than two centuries and a quarter that secure position has remained unimpaired, with results which are well known, and upon which it is not in the smallest degree necessary to enlarge.

But, vital as the independence of judges has always been, there never was a time when it was more manifestly important than in these latter days, when the effect of so much that the Executive does or permits is to render it difficult for the Courts to maintain the rights of the individual. The method of attack, to be sure, is subtle enough. In Tudor and in Stuart times much was attempted in defiance of Parliament. The attempts ultimately failed, and failed signally. But despotism may be no less sinister, and perhaps even more mischievous, if it acts under the cloak of Parliamentary forms than when it seeks to act in direct opposition to Parliament. Let it be granted that there may be acute and well-intentioned persons who have persuaded themselves that the rights of individuals are perfectly safe in the hands of Government departments, and may properly and economically be left to be determined behind the back of one of the parties, by officials of the Executive, upon principles not to be explained. But that is not, or at any rate is not yet, the general view in this country, nor is it likely to become the general view if the relevant facts are sufficiently well known. Meantime, however, judicial decision may often appear to be a stumbling-block in the way of the zealous official. The official course might be so much more smooth, and the official arm might be so much more powerful, if there were no troublesome Law Courts to stand between the Executive and the individual, the Crown and the taxpayer.

It is not enough, therefore, that Parliament and the public should be unceasingly vigilant to observe and to destroy clauses in Bills which, if they are enacted, have the effect of placing some departmental decision or other beyond the reach of the law. It is necessary also to be astute to preserve judicial independence against any assault, however insidious. A good example of the insidious kind of assault is to be found in the scheme, which raised its head in public a little time ago, and is by no means defunct to-day, for the destruction of the profoundly important office of Lord Chancellor. Nobody who has given any thought to the matter is likely to deny that the special and peculiar position of the Lord Chancellor is most intimately connected with the independence of the judges. One of his duties, and one of the most important of them, is to preside over the ultimate tribunal of appeal. It is obviously necessary, therefore, as indeed the statute requires, that he should be qualified by long experience in the study and the practice of the law. As a rule, of course, he has previously held the office of Attorney-General, the head of the Bar of England. And it is upon this eminent lawyer, nurtured and trained in law, and in the traditions of that Bar with which he has been long and honourably associated, that the critical task from time to time devolves of selecting the member of the Bar whom he is to recommend for appointment by the King to a vacant seat on the Bench in the Supreme Court of Judicature. For that high duty he has every qualification, and he performs that duty not only with the most conscientious care but also with the most intimate knowledge of those who come within the field of choice, and with the deepest respect for the spirit, the traditions, and the duties of the Bar. But the scheme is to get rid of him, to parcel out his functions among various individuals, and in particular to assign the duty of making judicial appointments to a new Minister, who is to be named the Minister of Justice.

Now, the name "Minister of Justice" would be new in England. But it is well known in some countries where the position of judges is very different from the position of English judges, and where the legal system is very different from our own. It is not necessary to consider or to criticize the systems which prevail in those countries, or any of them. But it is to be observed that, under the scheme which is proposed, it is not intended that the new Minister of Justice, if and when he is appointed, should preside over the ultimate tribunal of appeal, or perform any other judicial duties. It is not intended that he should be qualified to perform any duties of the kind, or indeed that legal training of any sort should be a necessary qualification for the office. But into the hands of that Minister it is proposed to gather up all the powers of making recommendations for appointment to judicial office, by whomsoever those powers may now be exercised. The post of Minister of Justice would be upon the same plane with other posts in the Government, and would be open to general competition among rising or risen politicians.

A man does not need to be a pessimist in order to foresee the natural and probable consequences of such a method, if it were ever established. Sooner or later, and rather sooner than later, it is to be expected that the office of Minister of Justice would be held by somebody who, without the smallest disrespect, might be described as a mere politician. His interest in law, and in the traditions of the law, would be neither more nor less than that of any other member of the Cabinet. Instead of being at one and the same time a member of the Judiciary, profoundly conscious of his duties to the Judiciary, and a member of the Executive, profoundly conscious of his duties to the Executive, he would be a member of the Executive alone. To put the matter in another way, appointments to the Judicial Bench would be in the hands of an ordinary political Minister, a stranger to legal training, and having little knowledge of contemporary members of the Bar except by accident or hearsay. Does anybody fail to perceive what, in the long run, would be likely to happen? From time to time, as every lawyer knows, the Judicial Bench, even as things stand, has suffered the disadvantage of political appointments. No doubt the pressure of Whips and the claims of meritorious political lieutenants have very often been resisted. But nobody who is at all aware of the inner workings of the political machine can be ignorant that pressure of this kind is frequently and forcibly employed. It is resisted, and can with firmness be resisted, by a Lord Chancellor whose knowledge of the Bar is personal and intimate, and who has every inclination and incentive to maintain the highest standard of judicial competence. It is not many years ago since a certain Lord Chancellor, when a Cabinet colleague entered his room, addressed him in some such words as these: "Now, I know exactly what you have come about; you have come to urge me to appoint one of the Government's supporters in the House of Commons to the vacant judgeship; you will not, I assure you, mention his name to me unless indeed you wish to prejudice his chances; I am perfectly willing to believe that every one of my colleagues in the Cabinet has in his pocket, or up his sleeve, the name of at least one member of

Parliament who, in his opinion, is a fit and proper person to be appointed to the Bench". The rebuke, for such it was, and was intended to be, had on that occasion the desired effect. But how much more difficult it would be for a purely political Minister to take such a stand, and how much less likely he would be to take it.

But the real danger, it may be thought, is something far more perilous and far more insidious than the danger of what are now called political appointments. The Minister of Justice, under the scheme which is suggested, might not only be a politician who had no special acquaintance with law or lawyers; he would also, of course, and of necessity, like the rest of his colleagues in the Government, be a bird of passage, and when the Government came to an end his tenure of office would automatically be terminated. Under our present system, with the Lord Chancellor at its head, there is a strong guarantee not only of independent personal knowledge but also of something like continuity. Every Lord Chancellor, by the nature of things, is well acquainted with the attainments of most, at any rate, of the leading members of the Bar. To say nothing of many other channels of information, including the reports of decided cases which he knows so well, he actually hears many of the members of the Bar in the conduct of cases before the House of Lords, sitting as the final Court of Appeal. He has lived, and to a great extent still lives, in a legal atmosphere. He is able, from actual personal knowledge, and his own skilled and experienced judgement, to assess the relative merits of conceivable candidates for judicial appointment. And when one Lord

Chancellor goes, another Lord Chancellor, who in his turn has the advantage of personal knowledge and professional equipment, succeeds to the office. In the result, there is never a time when a judicial vacancy cannot be filled by the exercise of the direct personal choice of a highly qualified lawyer, relying absolutely upon his own independent knowledge and authority. The contrast between this state of facts and the state of facts which would assuredly be brought into existence under a Minister of Justice who was a layman is at once startling and complete. Layman would succeed layman, with no more than a layman's knowledge of the Bar. He would not have the opportunity, even if he had the capacity, to test the merit of members of the Bar by personal observation, for the reason that he would not, as he could not, adjudicate in any Court. Where, then, would the real authority come to reside? Where, if anywhere, would be the reservoir of accumulated experience to which recourse must be had whenever the duty of making a judicial appointment had to be discharged? The answer is perfectly obvious. The experience, such as it might be, would be found, and the decisive authority would undoubtedly rest, in the permanent officials who surrounded the Minister. In those days, if they should ever dawn, some permanent official in the Ministry of Justice, if he were asked by a judicial visitor from the other side of the Atlantic, "Tell me, who really selects the judges in England?" might answer in no mere mood of post-prandial expansiveness, but as matter of actual and sober fact, "I am the person who really selects them. The Minister of Justice is but a transient, embarrassed phantom, here to-day and gone to-morrow. But I am always here. Mine is the knowledge, mine the experience, and the task of the Minister is simply to ratify my decision."

To say nothing of the hundred other objections to any such scheme or makeshift, it may be well to mention two. All experience shows that nothing is more dangerous in public affairs than that nominal responsibility should belong to one person while real authority rests with another. Where that method or condition exists the person who has the real authority is tempted from time to time to act in a way in which he certainly would not act if he had, and was known to have, the public responsibility. On the other hand, the person who has the public responsibility is tempted from time to time, in haste or in ignorance or in a variety of other circumstances, to act in a way in which he would never think of acting if he had real authority,—and afterwards to improvise excuses. Nothing could be more sinister, nothing could be more odious, than that any such division of powers should be erected into a system in the crucially important matter of making judicial appointments. But there is another grave objection which it is not possible to pass over in silence. If this evil thing, which it is desired to make public and thereby to prevent, were indeed to be perpetrated, the appointment of the Judiciary would sooner or later, and, again rather sooner than later, be in the unfettered hands of the bureaucracy itself. It is not necessary to attempt to forecast and to enumerate the manifold mischiefs which would not merely in all probability but of necessity follow. It must, however, be quite obvious to anyone who takes the trouble to think the matter out that the status and the position of the judges would certainly undergo a disastrous change; that the standing and calibre of members of the Bar who were ready and willing to accept judicial office would gradually be transformed; and that in the great and growing contest between the rights of the citizen and the pretensions of the bureaucrat there would come to be a complete and revolutionary change of forces. Nobody who is aware of the relevant facts could dream for a moment that the public, with its eyes open, would willingly embrace a peril so menacing. The danger is that the change may be plausibly made while the public is not yet aware, or is looking the other way.

The terms employed by despotism at different times and in different circumstances may vary, but its methods, upon analysis, prove to be rather monotonously similar. Everybody remembers, for example, the earlier history of interference by the Executive with the judges. In the reign of James I., one Peacham, a minister in Somersetshire, was prosecuted for high treason. A sermon, never preached, had been found in his study, which contained censures on the King and invectives against the Government. He was put to the rack, but no explanation could be drawn from him as to his design in writing the sermon. The writing of the sermon was relied upon as an overt act of compassing the King's death. The King directed Bacon to confer with the judges of the King's Bench, one by one, beforehand, in order to secure their determination for the Crown. Sir Edward Coke, Chief Justice of the King's Bench, objected that "such particular" and, as he called it, "auricular taking of opinions" was not "according to the custom of this realm". The other three judges, having been tampered with, agreed to answer such questions concerning the case as might be put to them. Coke continued to maintain his objection to this separate closeting of judges, but, finding himself abandoned by his colleagues, consented to give answers in writing, which seem to have been merely evasive. Peacham was found guilty, but not executed. He died in prison a few months afterwards.

A little later, the validity of a grant of a benefice to a bishop to be held *in commendam* came into question in a cause in the King's Bench, and the King, on hearing that his prerogative of making such a grant was disputed, signified to the Chief Justice, through the Attorney-General, that he would not have the Court proceed to judgement till he had spoken with them. Coke requested that similar letters might be written to the judges of all the Courts. This step having been taken, the judges assembled, and, by a letter subscribed by all of them, certified His Majesty that they were bound by their oaths not to regard any letters that might come to them contrary to law, but to do the law notwithstanding, that they held with one consent the Attorney-General's letter to be contrary to law, and such as they could not yield to, and that they had proceeded according to their oath to argue the cause. The King, then at Newmarket, replied (*inter alia*) that their oath not to delay justice was not meant to prejudice the King's prerogative, and commanded them to forbear meddling any further with the cause till they should hear his pleasure from his own mouth. On the King's return to London, the twelve judges were summoned to the Council Chamber, and harangued by the King with respect both to the substance and to the form of their letter. The judges, it was said, ought to check those advocates who presumed to argue against his prerogative, which ought not to be disputed or handled in vulgar argument. As to the form of the letter, instead of certifying him merely what they had done, they should have submitted to his princely judgement what they should do. The judges fell on their knees, and acknowledged their error as to the form of the letter. But Coke entered on a defence of the substance, maintaining the delay required to be against the law and their oaths. After consultation with the Chancellor and the Attorney-General, who delivered opinions opposed to those of Coke, the following question was put to the judges:

> "Whether, if at any time, in a case depending before the judges, His Majesty conceived it to concern him either in power or profit, and thereupon required to consult with them, and that they should stay proceedings in the meantime, they ought not to stay accordingly?"

All, except Coke, declared that they would do so, and acknowledged it to be their duty. Coke answered only that, when the case should arise he would do what should be fit for a judge to do. Coke was suspended from his office, and not long afterwards dismissed, though he was restored in about three years to the Privy Council.

Again, before assenting to the Petition of Right, Charles I. had a conference with the judges and put the following question (*inter alia*) to them:

> "Whether, if the King grant the Commons' petition, he doth not thereby exclude himself from committing or restraining a subject for any time or cause whatsoever without showing a cause?"

The answer of the judges was:

> "Every law, after it is made, hath its exposition, and so this petition and answer must have an exposition as the case in the nature thereof shall require to stand with justice; which is to be left to the Courts of Justice to determine, which cannot particularly be discovered until such case shall happen. And although the petition be granted, there is no fear of conclusion as is intimated in the question."

Afterwards, Charles I. issued writs for ship-money, directing the sheriffs to assess every landholder and other inhabitant according to their judgement of his means, and to enforce the payment by distress. The greater part yielded, but symptoms of opposition appeared in some places. The judges of assize were directed to inculcate on their circuits the necessary obligation of forwarding the King's service by complying with his writ. But as the measure grew more obnoxious, and strong doubts of its legality came more to prevail, it was thought expedient to publish an extra-judicial opinion of the twelve judges, taken at the King's special command. They gave it as their unanimous opinion that

> "when the good and safety of the kingdom in general is concerned, and the whole kingdom in danger, His Majesty might, by writ under the great seal, command

> all his subjects, at their charge, to provide and furnish such number of ships, with men, munitions, and victuals, and for such time as he should think fit, for the defence and safety of the kingdom; and that by law he might compel the doing thereof, in case of refusal or refractoriness; and that he was the sole judge, both of the danger, and when and how the same was to be prevented and avoided."

When the case of Hampden came before the twelve judges, sitting as the Exchequer Chamber, however, there was a majority of no more than seven to five in favour of the Crown, the Chief Justice of the King's Bench (Brampston) and the Chief Baron of the Exchequer (Davenport) being among the judges who decided in Hampden's favour. The judgement for the Crown was, of course, afterwards annulled by the Long Parliament.

Upon the ancient malpractice of consulting the judges beforehand, it may be interesting to add three passages. The first is from Lingard's *History of England* (4th ed., vol. v. p. 282):

> "In 1486 Humphrey Stafford, who had fled for sanctuary to the Church of Colnham, an obscure village near Abingdon, was taken from the Church by force, and brought to Worcester, to be executed for treason in virtue of an Act of Attainder previously passed against him, but the abbot of Abingdon arrived on the same day and required that he should be replaced in the sanctuary. This saved his life for the time. He was sent to the Tower and the judges were consulted by the King (Hen. VII.) whether Colnham had the privilege of a sanctuary. They replied it was hard and contrary to order that they

should give their opinions beforehand on a matter on which they would have to decide judicially. Henry assented with reluctance; the point was argued before all the judges; and the claim of sanctuary was rejected."

The second passage is from Lodge's *Portraits* (iii. 135):

"Sir Walter Raleigh, 1617. After the solemn mockery of a conference held by all the judges, he was, on the 28th October, brought to the King's Bench bar, and required to say why execution of the sentence passed on him fifteen years before should not now be awarded; defended himself with a vigour of argument and beauty of eloquence which astonished all who heard him; and was the next day, under the authority of a special warrant signed by the King, beheaded in Old Palace Yard, Westminster."

The third passage is from Lodge's *Illustrations of British History* (iii. pp. 171-173). It is part of a letter from Sir Thomas Edmonds to the Earl of Shrewsbury:

". . . The Judges have, of late met at Maidenhead, to consider of the crimes of the prisoners; and, as I understand, they make no question of finding them all culpable, save only Sir Walter Raleigh, against whom it is said that the proofs are not so pregnant: Serjeant Harris hath been this day called before the Lords about 'those busynes', but I do not yet see any liklihood that he will prove much fault. . . . My Lord Chief Justice and the King's Counsel are appointed to be here to-morrow to confer with the Lords about the further proceedings against the prisoners, which we conceive will not be long deferred. . . . From the Court at Woodstock, in haste, the eleventh of September, 1603."

Nor is it to be forgotten that all the Stuart Kings claimed the right to legislate by proclamation. In the time of James I. the practice of issuing proclamations interfering with the liberty of the subject, in cases not provided for by Parliament, had grown more usual than under Elizabeth. Coke was sent for to attend some of the Council, and was asked whether the King, by his proclamation, might prohibit new buildings about London, and whether he might prohibit the making of starch from wheat. Coke replied that the King could not change any part of the common law, nor create any offence by his proclamation which was not an offence before, without Parliament; but that it was a matter of great importance, on which he would confer with his brethren. This course was agreed to by the Council, and three judges, as well as Coke, were appointed to consider the matter. They resolved "that the King, by his proclamation, cannot create any offence which was not one before; for then he might alter the law of the land in a high point; for if he may create an offence where none is, upon that ensues fine and imprisonment". It was also resolved that the King hath no prerogative but what the law of the land allows him; but the King, for the prevention of offences, "may by proclamation admonish all his subjects that they keep the laws and do not offend them, upon punishment to be inflicted by the law"; and the neglect of the proclamation aggravates the offence. Lastly, they resolved that "if an offence be not punishable in the Star Chamber, the prohibition of it by proclamation cannot make it so".

The proclamations of the reign of Charles I. were far

more numerous than those of his father. They imply a prerogative of intermeddling with all matters of trade, prohibiting or putting under restraint the importation of various articles, and the growth of others at home, or establishing regulations for manufactures. Prices of certain minor articles were fixed by proclamation, and in one instance this restriction was extended to poultry, butter, and coals. It was declared that the King had incorporated all tradesmen and artificers in London and three miles round; so that no person might set up any trade, without having served a seven years' apprenticeship, and without admission into the corporation.

More than that, it was generally understood to be an ancient prerogative of the Crown to dispense with penal statutes in favour of particular persons, and under certain restrictions. The King might, by a *nolle prosequi*, stop any criminal prosecution commenced in his Courts, though not an action for the recovery of a penalty given to a common informer. He might set at liberty by means of a pardon any person imprisoned, whether upon conviction or by a magistrate's warrant. But Charles II., by his Declaration of Indulgence, purported to suspend all penal laws in matters ecclesiastical. The House of Commons voted that the King's prerogative, in matters ecclesiastical, did not extend to repeal Acts of Parliament; and addressed the King to recall his Declaration. In his answer to this address, the King lamented that the House should question his ecclesiastical power, a course which had never been taken before. In a second address the Commons positively denied the right of the King to suspend any law. At length the King gave way, and withdrew his Declaration.

A collusive action (*Godden* v. *Hales*) was brought in the reign of James II. to test the right of the Crown to dispense with the Test Act. Sir Edward Hales was a Roman Catholic, and the action was brought in the name of his servant to recover the penalty of £500 imposed by the Test Act for accepting the commission of colonel of a regiment without the previous qualification of receiving the sacrament in the Church of England. The King had privately secured the opinion of the Bench in his favour before the action was brought, and the prerogative was upheld by eleven judges to one. Herbert, C.J., laid down that there was no law that might not be dispensed with by the supreme lawgiver; though it was generally agreed among lawyers that the King could not dispense with the common law, nor with any statute prohibiting that which was *malum in se*, nor with any right or interest of a private person.

Soon afterwards James issued his famous declaration for liberty of conscience, suspending the execution of all penal laws concerning religion, and freely pardoning all offences against them, in as full a manner as if each individual had been named. He declared also his will and pleasure that the oaths of supremacy and allegiance, and the several tests enjoined by statutes of the late reign, should no longer be required of anyone before his admission to offices of trust. It was this declaration, and the prosecution of the Bishops for refusing to publish it, that led directly to the Revolution.

The most recent case in which the attempt was made, not merely to obtain the opinions of His Majesty's judges beforehand, but actually to establish by statute a system whereby the judges would be ordered and required to give their opinions beforehand, behind the back of one of the parties, is afforded by the Rating and Valuation Bill of 1928—a Government measure. The proposal which that Bill contained, and the protests which it excited in the House of Lords in April 1928, seem to be well worthy of the closest attention. The clause is accordingly set out in full, and is followed by passages from some of the speeches which it provoked. In the form in which the Bill left the House of Commons it contained a certain clause 4, entitled "decisions of doubtful points of law", which was in the following terms:

> "4. (1) If on the representation of the Central Valuation Committee, made after consultation with such associations or bodies as appear to them to be concerned, it is made to appear to the Minister of Health that a substantial question of law has arisen in relation to the valuation of hereditaments or of any class of hereditaments for the purposes of rating and that, unless that question is authoritatively determined, want of uniformity or inequality in valuation may result, the Minister may submit the question to the High Court for its opinion thereon, and the High Court, after hearing such parties as it thinks proper, shall give its opinion on the question.
>
> "(2) The Central Valuation Committee may appear as parties on the hearing of any such case for the purpose of supporting any contention with respect to the ques-

tion at issue and may, if they think fit so to do, contribute such amount as they think proper towards the costs of any persons appearing on the hearing for the purpose of supporting the contrary contention."

In the discussion in Committee in the House of Lords, speeches were made from which the following passages may be cited:

LORD HANWORTH: ". . . The clause is a specious one. It purports to give an opportunity to the Central Valuation Committee, who are charged with most responsible and difficult duties, to obtain the solution of intricate points which may arise in the course of the rating of certain properties, and this clause would, as it stands, propose to solve problems that may arise and explain certain difficulties. It was pointed out, when this clause was under consideration on the Second Reading, that it will not effect that purpose without impinging upon the rights of a great number of persons who may be interested.

"It is all very well to declare that the Minister of Health may, in difficulties which are abundantly explained in the opening part of the clause, submit a question to the High Court for its opinion thereon, and, to the layman, it might be supposed that it is perfectly legitimate for the Minister to obtain an opinion and that that opinion would be of value. It would be of value, but it might be of great injustice to many others who are not bound by it. The effect of this clause is to enable a Minister to submit a question to the High Court and to obtain an opinion. When that opinion is obtained the Minister will be armed with an authoritative declaration which, it might be said, he could apply in all cases. A judgement of the Court is binding upon the parties, and it is of authority where the facts are similar and in analogous cases, but it is quite a new thing for the Minister to be able to secure an opinion which can afterwards be held *in terrorem* over others who may have cases somewhat similar. For my part—and I think all lawyers will agree upon this—it is quite irregular and unwise that this power should be given to the Ministry, because it might be used (and there is a danger of its being used) in cases where it does not apply, thus preventing those who desire to have their matters decided on their own proper facts from bringing those matters to the attention of the Court in the ordinary way. Personally I am absolutely against the clause altogether."

LORD MERRIVALE: ". . . It is a really mischievous clause. I am not concerned with the matters which are here raised. I am not concerned in public administration, and I am not one of any body of judges likely to be resorted to when any question arises under this Bill in respect of rating law. I hope I am as disinterested in the matter as any member of your Lordships' House, but I have had acquaintance with the practical working of these things.

"I have, at any rate, this qualification, that through a long professional life I was often engaged in such matters as here arise, and in various judicial capacities in later times I was concerned with the decision of such questions, and in the personal position of a ratepayer I know how this class of legislation operates. With this knowledge I have the strong conviction that on the whole this clause, in the form in which it is presented, is a mischievous clause. What it would effect, whether it is designed or not, would be to make the Judiciary act in an ancillary and advisory capacity to the Executive, and confound the working of the judicial system with Executive administration. Every student of politics who has considered the matter during the whole of our political history has seen that that is the road to mischief. It was the kind of proposal, the kind of intention, which led to the removal of Lord Coke from his high office, and to his going into opposition against the then Government (which, of course, had an autocratic flavour about it, but which he had honestly as an Englishman supported), because, as he said, it established a species of auricular relation between His Majesty's Administration and the judges, who had to be impartial in all questions affecting the subject.

"When this clause is examined, what will be seen is that the department in question, where it is anticipated that grave difficulties may arise, will be able to select a general question of law, a question of general application, to get the sanction of the Minister of Health for proceeding under this clause, and then to take care that, upon a question and with a process of argument which will be regulated by itself, it will anticipate a conflict of authority with the individual by securing, upon arguments which it controls, a decision of a judge which is intended to be authoritative and secure in advance. There is nothing like it in the whole character of our law. I do not know that there is anything like it in the character of the law of any Western State. I have not enough experience of the latest developments of autocratic government to know if elsewhere there is some process by which, when the citizen comes to be in conflict with the Executive, he must go to the department with which he is in conflict and elicit from some pigeonhole in which it is placed for reference a decision which they say governs the situation. This is totally contrary to anything that we have known of in the whole history of administration in this country, and for my part I confess that I regard it with great apprehension. I know that it is proposed with the best intention by Ministers who desire simplicity of administration and certainty in the application of the law, but this is not the mode by which it is to be got.

"There is not really any difficulty in securing the opinion of the Courts at a minimum of expense upon a case stated with regard to any question which arises in practice. As soon as there is a dispute and litigation, the authorities are in a position, by one or other of the processes provided either in Quarter Sessions practice or in the practice of the High Court, to agree what the facts are, to bring them before a judge, and to argue the question. That is the businesslike, safe, and sensible way in which this class of matter has been dealt with in past times, and the result has been to attach to the judicial decision a degree of confidence which, outside this country, is almost unheard of. It is known that the Judiciary have no particular association with the Executive, that they are not approached by the Executive with a view to their coming to conclusions that the Executive desire, that there are not any auricular communications between them, as Lord Coke said, that the thing will have been fairly thought out, and that a decision arrived at in that way falls into the body of the law and guides the opinion of everybody who is concerned.

"That is the old process, the existing process, and it can be pursued quite simply now. Steps could be taken by means of which a department could be put in a position to intervene and to take care that there was a thorough discussion and that its views were represented. But a system which puts a public department in a position to take charge of the question with which it deems itself administratively concerned, to organize the argument of it, to provide payment according to its views for some of the argument, to obtain a decision and then to promulgate or to retain it to regulate its relations with His Majesty's subjects is unheard of. I believe such a system is very unhealthy, and for my part I regret that it, or anything like it, is found in this Bill.

"I want to say two or three words more with regard to the position of His Majesty's judges in this matter. It is no part of the business of His Majesty's judges, and never has been part of their business, at any rate since the Act of Settlement, to have any advisory concern in the acts of the Administration, or to take any part in advising the Administration. The natural effect of associating them with the Administration and attaching to them the responsibility for conclusions which are put forward by the Administration will be to weaken the authority of the Judiciary. It can have no other effect. As I have said, this is no part of the business of a judge. The business of a judge is regulated by his oath of office. It is to determine according to law, without fear, favour, or affection, questions which arise between His Majesty's subjects or between any of His Majesty's subjects and either the Throne or the Executive. That is the function of the judges. Why should the judges be brought in by this side-wind to help the Executive to carry on their business, to replace the Law Officers and to relieve the Executive of responsibility as to decisions that they ought to arrive at upon the law?

"This is not a fair proposal with regard to the Executive, and I ask those of His Majesty's Ministers who know how business is done in the law whether they think that any judge whose opinion is worth having is going to be a party to a system of obtaining opinions in advance of litigation by processes such as this Bill makes possible, or whether, on the other hand, when a case of this kind comes for opinion in advance and is presented to a judge who understands his business—which I think may be said of all His Majesty's judges—he will not say: 'I have not any facts before me as to this abstract question. It will depend upon facts and the conclusion may be this way or that way, but when I see the facts to which it is desired that the opinion shall be applied I shall be able to express an opinion with regard to those facts.'

"An opinion with regard to any dispute on facts can be obtained now. Why is it that, in terms exceedingly difficult of application and almost impossible to justify from the point of view of practical experience, we get this proposal for a resort by the Executive at its choice and under its authority to the judges, with power given to demand of a judge, whose business it is to decide disputes between them and His Majesty's subjects, some opinion in advance which may have the effect of unjustly concluding those disputes?"

Viscount Haldane: "My Lords, in the debate which took place upon this Bill, and particularly upon this clause, before Easter, there was disclosed very considerable repugnance on the part of the House to accept clause 4, and I think that the discussion this afternoon shows that that repugnance has not abated. At the bottom of it all there is a question of principle. The clause is an attempt to introduce something quite novel, so far as the law of England is concerned, into our procedure—to introduce the plan of enabling an abstract question, a question not necessarily relating to any concrete case but purely general, to be put before the judges, and the judges are to be compelled—the word is 'shall'—to give an opinion upon that question. That plan is unknown to our law. On the last occasion the noble and learned Earl opposite referred to the *responsa prudentum* of the Romans as a sort of precedent. I had already spoken, and therefore could not answer, but that system, by which the Romans liked to get opinions given by wise and highly competent outsiders on general questions, is a system which is absolutely unknown to the jurisprudence of this country. We have nothing whatever to do with it.

"Here the system is that if two people dispute they can carry the concrete fact before the Court, and upon that concrete fact the Court can decide, and the Court does not go beyond that, unless it be necessary to lay down principles in arriving at a decision. We have not had experience of the other procedure. I referred on the last occasion to the liking which had grown up in Canada for submitting abstract constitutional questions to the Courts there and ultimately to the Privy Council. In my opinion experience of that course has led to enormous inconvenience, and successive Lords Chancellor have objected to and denounced it. The late Lord Herschell said some strong things about it, and at times refused to give an opinion. The late Lord Loreburn was even stronger, and other Lords Chancellor and other judges in the Judicial Committee have expressed themselves without restraint upon a system which they deemed to be very mischievous. It was mischievous because it invited the Court to go beyond the particular case which it had to decide, and to say things beyond the facts to which the decision would be applied, which might prejudice future suitors.

"That is what is proposed to be done here. The Minister, if he thinks fit, is to ask the Court to give an opinion upon what may be a purely abstract question, and then when the Court has given its opinion, which it has got to do, because the word used is 'shall', obviously that opinion is to be used as an authoritative guide to the Court on the next occasion. I can only say, judging from the experience which I myself have had, that such a procedure is very embarrassing to future litigants. It involves them in a great deal of confusion, and leaves them without certainty whether the law laid down in perfectly general terms will or will not deprive them of rights which they think they possess. I think this clause is an objectionable one. I think it is an objectionable one also as drawing the judges into the region of administration, and I cannot but feel that the Government would be well advised not to press the clause, to which it is obvious that in this House there is a great deal of repugnance felt, and which I am sure will be regarded with a great deal of repugnance by experienced lawyers outside."

LORD ATKIN: ". . . This power is taken by the department to assist in a rapid, easy, and cheap determination of points which they think it is necessary should be determined. I am not satisfied that if this duty is confided to the Judiciary they will perform it willingly, and on the other hand there are practical difficulties. I should like to point out that it is now admitted that the proposal is one that does conflict with what has been for generations the principle upon which justice has been administered in His Majesty's Courts—namely, that they decide questions that have actually arisen between subject and subject or subject and the Crown. They have not in the past had as part of their duty to advise a department upon questions of law that did not arise in the manner that I have said. . . . What is the position here? The Minister contemplates that he may instruct counsel and the Central Valuation Committee may appear as parties. Therefore they will be liable for costs. But the Central Valuation Committee have no funds of their own. The only funds they have are voluntary funds which may be paid to them by the different rating authorities. They may not be able to pay even their own costs, but they certainly have no power of calling upon the funds of assessment committees for the purpose of paying the costs of the persons who may be opposing them. The real difficulty is that there is no sufficient protection given to those persons whose interests are contrary to those which may correspond to the view taken by the Central Valuation Committee."

On a later day further discussion took place:

LORD MERRIVALE: ". . . This is a fundamental and constitutional change in judicial administration in this country. Everybody who understands it knows that it is so. The question that I want to ask at some convenient time is as to what steps His Majesty's Government have taken to assure themselves that this grave proposed change can work. That is one thing that I want to know. The time is so short that, besides putting down this Question to-day, I have formulated a Motion for to-morrow. It seems an extravagant thing to do, but we know nothing about this matter. I have formulated a Motion to the effect that it is not fair to His Majesty's judges to put upon them this task, which is not part of their duty, which they have never engaged to perform, and which it is proposed to make a statutory duty. It is not fair so to treat a body of men like His Majesty's judges, some of whom, I have reason to believe, are satisfied that such a course would be mischievous as regards the general administration of justice. I have formulated a Resolution to this effect, and I have added that it is not consistent with the due administration of justice that a Minister who has obtained in advance an advisory opinion from a judge should afterwards bind His Majesty's subjects to that opinion although they were not parties to it. I do not think that anybody can say a word to the contrary of those two proposals, but they are both contradicted by clause 4 and we have had no sort of intelligible explanation why this is done, how it is to be carried out, what expectations His Majesty's Government had, and where this proposal originated.

"Let me tell my noble and learned friend that I am particularly concerned with regard to its origin, because I recall something that happened here on almost the last occasion when the late deeply-lamented holder of the office of Lord Chancellor was sitting in this House. There was a proposal to transfer all business by way of dispute between landlord and tenant under a highly contentious new Bill to a scratch tribunal, a committee, nominated nobody knew how, which was to take charge of all these matters and of the contentious affairs of His Majesty's subjects, without any opportunity of recourse to the Courts of Law to which everyone of His Majesty's subjects is entitled under our Constitution to go. We changed that Bill before Christmas with great difficulty. The Bill narrowly escaped being thrown out because of that clause. Consider this clause and associate it with that clause. I am afraid that somewhere, not in His Majesty's Government but in the offices where matters of this kind are considered, there is some ingenious gentleman who has never commanded practice at the Bar but has gained some acquaintance with theories of law and is associated with a coterie of persons who are at present steadily engaged in the effort to remove questions of conflict between citizens out of the jurisdiction of the Courts in order to transfer them to the decision of administrative authorities."

LORD CARSON: "My Lords, I am sorry to say that, through circumstances which I could not control, I was unable to be present here when the Committee stage of this Bill came before your Lordships. I did my best on the Second Reading to proclaim the reasons of my opposition to this very grave and unparalleled system, which it is sought to set up, of trying to rope in the Judiciary to the help of the Executive in their administrative capacity. Anything more dangerous or more unfair to the subject I cannot conceive. . . . I cannot imagine anything worse than for us to lay down that such a procedure should be taken as one which may be applied to many other matters. Just fancy applying it to the Finance Acts—to those complicated measures which raise all the taxes of the country. A case might be submitted to the judges as to whether under a particular clause certain persons should be taxed, and then, if they were advised that that is not the proper construction, they would be told: 'Oh, you were not there;

we have got judgment; that is what the Court say'. Anything more mischievous I cannot imagine."

LORD MERRIVALE: "My Lords, the discussion which has taken place relieves me of the necessity of asking your Lordships to divide upon the Motion of which I gave Notice. I take full account of what the noble Earl has said regarding the inconvenience of anything anticipatory of a Motion and Division to-morrow. My fear has been that it would not be possible to get this matter formulated until noble Lords came to a decision upon this question. But so far as I am concerned I have now discharged what I conceive to be my public duty of calling express attention to this matter and to the grounds upon which I object in the strongest way to the taking of advisory opinions from the judges. Having done that, I feel that I am entitled to ask leave to withdraw the Motion now and to say that to-morrow I do not feel disposed to ask that further attention should be given to this matter in anticipation of the debate which will no doubt take place, if it becomes necessary, on the Third Reading. But I would say that I hope His Majesty's Government—and I include my noble and learned friend on the Woolsack—will in the meantime regard this not as a matter which has cropped up in a department and about which they are at issue with some who are their usual opponents and some who are their usual supporters, but as a matter which is really a grave question of principle, and that, applying their minds to it, they will see whether it is worth while to depart from ancient practice and introduce a novel principle which many of us think would be fraught with danger."

On further consideration the Government decided to

drop the clause. In the course of a speech announcing the withdrawal, the LORD CHANCELLOR (Lord Hailsham) said on the 1st May 1928:—

> "It has seemed to us that there is another matter which is to be considered. Not only is it important that the Judiciary should be independent of the Executive, but it is also of vital importance that the public should be satisfied that the Judiciary and the Executive are independent. We have thought that the undoubted fact that members of your Lordships' House occupying high judicial positions have seriously and sincerely believed that this principle of independence was being infringed, necessarily must arouse doubt and distrust in the public mind and that it was far better that we should abandon the effort to obtain a power of this kind than that we should run any risk of an impression being created, rightly or wrongly, in the minds of the public that there was any connection being established between the Executive and the Judiciary and any infringement of that independence of the Judiciary which is the palladium of the liberty of the subject.
>
> "In those circumstances, while from some points of view we regret the decision to which we have been obliged to come, the Minister of Health has authorised me to take such course as I think right to take in all the circumstances, and I have taken the responsibility, as in a sense combining the Judiciary and the Executive, of saying that the Government will not proceed with this clause and will ask the assent of the House that it should be dropped."

The following passages are cited from the speeches which followed:—

VISCOUNT HALDANE: "My Lords, the Lord Chancellor

has excellently acquitted himself of the dark suspicion of conspiracy which has been mooted against him and the Government. I never believed in that conspiracy, nor did I believe in the machinery which was supposed to have brought about the present situation. But what I did suspect and what I see very clearly now is the zeal of an administrative body who thought: 'Here is the most convenient way of solving all our doubts; we will pass a clause making the judges a sort of general legal advisers of the Government on abstract principles and will go to them and get rulings which will be of high authority'. I do not believe those rulings would have that high authority. I do not believe they ever would have been recognised as equivalent to judgments of the Courts. Therefore, I think it was a very poor piece of machinery even had it passed. But now the Lord Chancellor has spoken, as I say, excellently, for he is not only proposing to withdraw a clause which caused many of us a great deal of anxiety and caused a great deal of dislike to it on the part of people outside, but he has also emphasised that most important principle that the Judiciary in this country should stand between the subject and the Crown and should be the protectors of the subject in matters in which claims may be made, which may or may not be right but which ought to be adjudicated upon by an absolutely independent and fearless body. I think the course taken is a step in strengthening that which is a fundamental principle of this country, a principle which ought to be departed from in the way of seeking to substitute anything for the ordinary litigation of the country only very sparingly, and I congratulate the Government on having taken a wise decision, although somewhat late in the day."

Lord Merrivale: "My Lords, if I may be permitted three or four sentences I shall not exceed that length of speech. I am so gratified by what I think the wise decision of His Majesty's Government upon a question which I thought affected most gravely some of our higher public interests that I do not propose to spend one minute, or any part of a minute, in discussing the method by which His Majesty's Government have arrived at that wise decision. I cannot help thinking if my noble and learned friend on the Woolsack had been in a position to address his mind to the argument relating to this matter on the several occasions upon which the objections which he now appreciates were impressed upon the Government without any effect, the House would have been spared the discussions, somewhat disagreeable to some of us who felt bound to take part in them, which the House had to listen to upon the Second Reading and in the Committee stage."

Lord Hanworth: "My Lords, as the learned Lord Chancellor was good enough to refer to my opposition to this clause, perhaps you will allow me to express my gratitude to him for having dropped it. My gratitude is of such a generous nature that I am not at all inclined to discuss the question whence the temptation came under which the Government fell, 'if ever, in temptation strong, they left the right path for the wrong'. We may leave it at that. It may be that the temptation came from the Central Committee. I care not. But the temptation came, and they now see that it was a temptation and they have gone back to the right path. I am not speaking for myself alone, for I have had an opportunity of speaking to a great number of judges on whom would have been laid the task of responding to this irksome and, as I think, dangerous duty. Speaking for them, I know they will be very gratified indeed to think that this clause has been dropped."

LORD HEWART: "My Lords, may I in a word or two join in the thanks which are being offered to the Lord Chancellor for the wise withdrawal of this clause. In the events which have happened it is not necessary that I should refer even in a word to the feelings which the clause excited in the minds of His Majesty's Judges of the King's Bench Division. It was without exception the worst clause of its kind which has ever appeared. I say that having in mind Section 29 of the Local Government Act of 1888, and Section 70 of the Local Government Act of 1894. The first of those sections led to two abortive decisions which were afterwards overruled. This was a proposal to convert His Majesty's Judges into departmental solicitors. I am glad that the proposal has been withdrawn, and as it has been withdrawn I would venture to hope that the Lord Chancellor may now turn his mind to the many cases in the past—I hope there are not going to be many cases in the future—in which a different method is employed, I do not say by a hidden hand, but what is obviously a concerted endeavour to subtract from the Law Courts important decisions, and to get those decisions made, behind the backs of the parties interested, by a Department or a Departmental Committee. I join in the congratulations which have been offered, and in the circumstances refrain from saying much that otherwise I should have had to say."

Lord Carson, in the passage cited above from his speech in Committee on the Bill, referred to his earlier speech delivered in the course of the debate on the Second Reading (27th March 1928). That speech dealt so forcibly with more than one matter closely connected with the present inquiry that it seems convenient to reproduce part of it here:—

LORD CARSON: ". . . I certainly wish to take the first opportunity that I have of speaking on this Bill to enter my absolute protest against clause 4 as at present framed. I am not at all surprised to be told that a vast number of questions have arisen for legal decision under the Act of 1925, because it was pointed out, when that Act was before this House, that it was full of many difficulties and some absurdities, and we were only given a day or two in which to pass it. Otherwise, we were told, the Constitution would tumble over and the House of Lords would for ever cease to exist. We accepted the situation, as we always do at the end of a Session with a Conservative Government in power.

"Therefore I am not at all surprised to be told that there are these objections, and that they must be got rid of in some kind of way. For the sake of uniformity, and I have no doubt with very good intentions, somebody hit upon clause 4. If somebody would invent an easy way of having matters decided in the Courts of Law without the expense that now occurs, I should be the very first to support him, but if there is one matter above all others that this House ought to take care that a Government should not be allowed to do, it is that they should not be allowed to take from litigants the right of decision by the Courts and the right to argue their cases before them. That is what this clause does. I do not know why there is this passion recently for either setting up autocratic bodies within a department, or setting up tribunals *ad hoc*, which now is the fashionable way. Only a few months ago the Landlord and Tenant Bill was before us. They tried (and this House did something to prevent it) to take away certain matters entirely from the Courts of Law by that Bill, which left a great deal for the Judiciary to legislate upon. The result has been that agents and solicitors, and people concerned, are all warning everybody that they ought to have no transactions under the Act until the meanings are explained by the Courts. Now the Government want to get over that sort of difficulty by simply saying that the Central Valuation Committee may go to the Minister of Health, show there is a very great question of law with regard to the rating of hereditaments, or a class of hereditaments, for decision, and to ask him to take the case up to the Courts and have it decided.

"In the old days, as I understood, and I had some experience as a Law Officer, if in framing your Bill you had any doubt about it, you sent it to the Law Officers, and the Government had the care and responsibility for their own legislation. But now what you are to do is this: you are, without having any concrete case or parties before you, to go to the Courts and ask for their opinion. When that opinion is given I am not sure what is to happen. It does not say in the clause. All it says is that: 'the High Court after hearing such parties as it thinks proper shall give its opinion on the question'. Is that opinion to affect people who have not been heard? Is it to affect a number of people who may come within a certain class, but who may think they may have entirely different rights? If not, of what value is it? If it is a mere departmental matter to help the department, then probably there is not very much harm in it; but does it mean that when John Jones, the friend to whom the noble Lord opposite referred, has a case to be considered, and goes up before the Court, he is to be told that there is already a decision which has been given? He will say: 'When was it made? Why was I not given notice of it?' Of course, they cannot give everybody notice of what is going to affect people upon these decisions being taken by the High Court.

"Who is to state the case? I suppose the Central Valuation Committee. Who is to agree the facts? and the deductions from the facts? It is all to be stated behind the backs of the ratepayers. It may be a very convenient thing for a Government to be able to come forward when a ratepayer objects and to say: 'Oh, you cannot do anything more, this is all closed; on such and such a morning we went before the Lord Chief Justice and one of his colleagues in the King's Bench Division, and it is all completely settled'. 'But', he says, 'I did not know anything about it'. 'Well', is the reply, 'you ought to have known, because everybody is presumed to know the law, and the law has been settled by this Court'. Who is to settle the case? And then, if the Central Valuation Committee do not like the decision of the Court, are they to be able to go to the Court of Appeal? Are they to be able to go to the House of Lords? There is nothing about that in the Bill. 'The Minister may submit the question to the High Court for its opinion thereon', but how much further the matter goes I do not know.

"This, to my mind, is the very worst kind of legislation you could have in the interest of the subject. I cannot discuss it now, because it will have to come on as a Committee matter, and I am only discussing it in general outline. But I do beg of noble Lords to go into the question and be prepared when the matter comes up in Committee. There is no reason in the world, if this is allowed to be the way of deciding questions, why exactly similar provisions should not be put into Finance Bills. The Commissioners of Taxes might say: 'Where we are assessing cases of excess profits we often have great difficulty; why not put in a clause in such cases providing that all you have to do is to state a case for the High Court?' I look with great apprehension on a clause like this, which, if put into Finance Acts, would take away from the taxpayer the right which he now has to challenge an assessment, which would then not be based on a general principle that may have been sanctioned by the Court. However, I have no intention whatever of opposing the Bill, which may or may not be useful—I will take that assurance from my noble and learned friend who moved the Second Reading; but I do hope that by the time the Bill comes on in Committee noble Lords will have taken some trouble to instruct themselves upon the far-reaching consequences of this legislation."

The clause accordingly perished and the particular attempt failed. But nothing can diminish the significance of the fact that the attempt was made. Hardly less significant was the memorable speech in which Lord Salisbury, speaking as Lord Privy Seal, endeavoured to cover the retreat of the Government. The speech was brief; it was a matchless revelation; it ought to become a *locus classicus*. Here it is in full:—

The LORD PRIVY SEAL (The Marquess of Salisbury):

"My Lords, I do not intend to take part in a debate which has been entirely confined up to now to lawyers except to say that I do think lawyers might sometimes consider the interest of suitors. Here is a provision put into the Bill with the object of saving expense to unfortunate ratepayers, and the only thing which the great lawyers can think of is whether some special theory of law and of administration is complied with, and they do not think of those interests which are so acutely felt by the suitors. I do not contend for a moment that the noble and learned Lords are not right in their contention. They probably are. They know far more about it than I do, but I do say it is a most singular circumstance how very difficult it is for poor people to get justice in this country because they cannot really afford it on account of the enormous expense. The expense is growing every day, and the result is, I am quite sure, that there is a great failure of justice to the suitor. Whether that is unavoidable I cannot say. It may be so, but I do wish when great judges address themselves to your Lordships on this subject, that they would take into consideration that side of the case."

The conclusion appears to be irresistible. It looks as if somebody—who can it have been?—had told Lord Salisbury, and he had believed the statement, that it is to the interest of "poor people" to have their causes decided behind their backs, upon hypotheses formulated in advance by the opposite side.

A clause of this kind was not entirely novel. But previous experience ought at least to have served as a warning.

Section 29 of the Local Government Act, 1888, had provided as follows:

> "If any question arises, *or is about to arise*, as to whether any business, power, duty, or liability is or is not transferred to any county council or joint committee under this Act, that question, without prejudice to any other mode of trying it, may, on the application of a chairman of quarter sessions, or of the county council, committee, or other local authority concerned, be submitted for decision to the High Court of Justice in such summary manner as subject to any rules of Court may be directed by the Court; and the Court, after hearing such parties and taking such evidence (if any) as it thinks just, *shall decide the question*."

The sequel was extremely interesting. Recourse was had to the machinery provided by this section in two cases—one in 1891, the other in 1894. The cases, reported in the Law Reports, are *Ex parte County Council of Kent and Council of Dover, Ex parte County Council of Kent and Council of Sandwich* (1891, 1 Q.B. 389) and *In re County Council of Herefordshire and Town Council of the Borough of Leominster* (1895, 1 Q.B. 43). In the former case Mr. Justice Vaughan Williams, as he then was, giving judgement, said (at p. 399):

> "We hope that the principle upon which these answers are given sufficiently appears. We may in some cases have been mistaken, owing to the exact facts not having been brought to our notice".

The remark was prophetic. In 1898 the decision in both cases was overruled in *Thetford Corporation* v. *Norfolk*

County Council (1898, 2 Q.B. 468). Giving judgement in the Court of Appeal in this later case (which was a real, not a hypothetical, case), Lord Justice Vaughan Williams said (at p. 483) that he was "fully satisfied" that his previous decision "was wrong", and that he had put a construction upon the material sections "which I am now satisfied they will not bear". Yet this expensive lesson seems to have been thrown away.

CHAPTER VIII

WHAT IS TO BE DONE?

Expressions of judicial opinion upon the present matter, and upon matters akin to it, have been frequent, and it may be useful to recall some characteristic examples. So long ago as 1893 Lord Justice Bowen, in a well-known judgement, used some plain words upon the essential necessity of a right of appeal from decisions of official persons. The case was *The Queen* v. *Justices of County of London and London County Council* (1893, 2 Q.B. 476), and was concerned with a question of appeal against a certain valuation for poor-rate. Lord Justice Bowen said (at p. 492):

> "What is the ordinary rule of construction when construing Acts of Parliament and other documents? It is, that if the language is ambiguous and admits of two views you must not adopt that view which leads to manifest public mischief. Here is a broad scheme of metropolitan taxation and rating by which the parochial ministerial officers are empowered in the first instance to place values on hereditaments for the purpose of taxation in the broad sense. In a free country the very essence of such a system must be that there should be an appeal to some body who can say whether those officers are doing what is just. If no appeal were possible, I have no great hesitation in saying that this would not be a desirable country to live in, where every

parochial officer might do as he liked in this matter. It is quite true that there is enough difficulty in appealing as it is; but if there is to be no appeal at all possible the system would be intolerable. Therefore it is of the essence, the pivot of the system, that there should be a right of appeal."

That opinion seems to be well worthy of attention when it is sought to estimate and to comprehend the various devices of bureaucracy to give departmental decisions the force of a statute, to prevent them from being reviewed by any process in a Court of Law, and to ensure that the mere fact that a departmental decision has been given must be treated as conclusive evidence that the requirements of the law have been duly fulfilled.

To take a later example, eighteen years ago (May 4, 1911) *The Times* reported, under the headings "Encroachments of the Executive: The Master of the Rolls on a Modern Danger", a speech which had been delivered on the previous evening in the City of London by Sir H. H. Cozens-Hardy, as he then was. The report was as follows:

"The Master of the Rolls, who with Mr. English Harrison, K.C., responded for the Bench and the Bar, said that time was when the great danger against which the Judicature had to guard was the encroachments of the Crown. Happily there was no longer that danger; but there was another danger which was much more real than that—namely, encroachment by the Executive. He had seen signs of attempts by the Executive to interfere with the Judiciary, and against all such attempts he thought he could pledge his colleagues and himself to offer a strenuous resistance (Cheers). There

> was another danger connected with the Executive. In recent years it had been the habit of Parliament to delegate very great powers to Government departments. The real legislation was not to be found in the Statute-book alone. They found certain Rules and Orders by some Government departments under the authority of the Statute itself. He was one of those who regarded that as a very bad system and one attended by very great danger. For administrative action generally meant something done by a man whose name they did not know, sitting at a desk in a Government office, very apt to be a despot if free from the interference of the Courts of Justice."

And a few months ago a Judge of the highest distinction, whose abilities have shone successively in the King's Bench, the Court of Appeal, and the House of Lords, referred, in a passage which it is permitted here to repeat, to "the flagrant clauses we have had making departments their own Courts, the vast mass of government by Regulation on top of legislation by Order in Council, and 'departmental Bills', the object of which is to shepherd us and regiment us more and more".

It might indeed be worth while to collect and marshal in chronological order the observations which have been made upon the matter in the course of judgements delivered in Court since the beginning of the present century. Nineteen years have passed since Lord Justice Farwell said in the Court of Appeal: "The Courts are the only defence of the liberty of the subject against departmental aggression." (See Law Reports, 1911, 1 K.B. at p. 424). It will not escape notice, nevertheless, that departmental aggression has not only not diminished, but, on the contrary, has in a marked degree increased during the past quarter of a century.

Side by side with these expressions of judicial opinion may be placed a passage from the admirable volume entitled *Cases in Constitutional Law*, by Mr. D. L. Keir and Mr. F. H. Lawson, which was published in 1928. The learned editors say (p. 143):

"It would give much more satisfaction if the entire supervisory jurisdiction of the central departments was exercised in public and according to judicial forms. One cannot help sympathizing with the unsuccessful litigant in *L.G.B.* v. *Arlidge*, or with members of local authorities who object to being surcharged by a bureaucratic auditor. At present our administrative justice is too much of the 'hole and corner' variety.

"It is also essential that the ordinary Courts shall retain ultimate control in respect of legality; any step which tended to deprive the subject of the protection of the Courts against illegal encroachment on his private rights would be against all the principles of English law and English government, and would imply a return to Star Chamber methods. But there is at the present time an unfortunate tendency, due perhaps partly to a desire to avoid the enormous costs incident to ordinary litigation, but partly, one fears, to bureaucratic impatience of any control, to oust the jurisdiction of the ordinary Courts entirely in administrative matters. It is not uncommon to find in the Statute-book provisions giving to a minister of the Crown power to decide conclusively and in the last resort questions of a quasi-judicial character. Now there can be no objection to such a provision if it merely implies that the minister's discretion is, so long as he keeps within the limits which the law allows, absolute. But it is in most cases quite clear, and the Courts have interpreted it to mean, that their jurisdiction is entirely ousted. A reference to the case of *Ex parte Ringer* (1909), 25 T.L.R. 718, will indicate the possible effects of such legislation. There a Divisional Court had to interpret s. 39 (3) of the Small Holdings and Allotments Act, 1908 (8 Edw. VII. c. 36). They held that their jurisdiction was completely ousted. The section ran as follows:

> 'An order (of the local authority) under this section shall be of no force unless and until it is confirmed by the Board (of Agriculture), and the Board may, subject to the provisions of the first schedule to this Act, confirm the order either without modification or subject to such modifications as they think fit, and an order when so confirmed shall become final and have effect as if enacted in this Act, and the confirmation by the Board shall be conclusive evidence that the requirements of this Act have been complied with, and that the order has been duly made and is within the powers of this Act.'

"Such a section was a standing invitation to the Board to exceed its powers."

If it be asked where the remedy is to be found for the mischief which is here deplored, the answer is not difficult. Is it too much to hope, in the first place, that the worst of the offending sections in Acts of Parliament may be repealed or amended? And, in the second place, is it not comparatively easy to prevent similar sections from being enacted in future? To this end what is necessary is simply a particular state of public opinion, and in order that that state of public opinion may be brought into existence what is necessary is simply a knowledge of the facts. At present, it is tolerably safe to suppose, only a small part of the electorate knows what has been and is being done, while it is a still smaller part that has any real appreciation of the meaning and effect of the statutory provisions which offer at once the occasion and the instrument of despotic power. Two methods at least may be adopted, easily and immediately, by those who desire to discourage the new despotism. One is to form in each House of Parliament a Committee, not too large, whose sole task it should be to examine every Bill, as it is introduced, for the purpose of observing whether and in what respects its provisions may have the effect of increasing the power of bureaucracy, and whether and by what contrivance that power is to be made irresponsible. Other Committees, no doubt, and other individuals examine and consider every Bill from various other special and particular points of view. But it seems to be at once highly desirable and by no means impracticable that the members of each House should provide from their own ranks a voluntary and unofficial Committee who would ask themselves with reference to every new measure: (1) Does it confer, expressly or by implication, fresh powers upon the bureaucracy, (2) if so, how does it seek to attain that end, and (3) is the method, or is the probable result, of such a kind that the fresh powers may evade either the control of Parliament or the jurisdiction of the Courts? Similarly, it seems to be at once highly desirable and by no means impracticable that some, at least, of the leading newspapers should regard it as one of the appointed duties of some able member of the editorial staff, not occasionally or at the suggestion of another, but regularly and as a matter of course, to subject every new Bill to a similar examination. If the Bill contains the ingredient which it is desired to detect, to expose, and to destroy, well-timed publicity and well-directed opposition should effect their purpose. It may well be that departmental orders and regulations are, to some extent, unavoidable. But why should they be made behind the back of Parliament? It may well be, too, that departmental decision is, within strict limits and for defined purposes, even desirable. But why should it be screened and withdrawn from examination by the Courts of Law? There may be many unsustainable reasons, but there is no good reason, why departmental officials should have, or seem to have, the power of legislating without Parliamentary authority, or of giving a decision which an aggrieved person is unable to submit to the test of judicial inquiry. In this field, also, as in other fields, prevention is better than cure. It appears to be quite inconceivable that, if public opinion were alert and active in the matter, and if Parliament and the Press were known to be deliberately vigilant in the task of exposing and preventing this particular mischief, there would continue to be the same readiness on the part of those who are responsible for the work of drafting Bills to insert provisions of the objectionable type. At present, to judge from the form in which so many Bills are presented, it looks as if there were in existence in some departmental pigeon-hole a collection of model clauses, capable of being fitted into measures of very different kinds, which, when they have been somehow steered through the Houses of Parliament, confer upon departmental officials a power to legislate not inferior to the powers of Parliament itself, and a power to pronounce unappealable decisions such as is neither possessed nor desired by a judicial tribunal.

Some steps, it may be thought, are tolerably obvious. Why should not the Rules Publication Act, in fact as well as in name, be "simplified and amended" so as to exclude exception or evasion, and so as to secure a real and effective Parliamentary supervision over all rules and orders? And it goes without saying that there should be an end of all schemes to enable Government departments to re-write a statute, or to invite premature opinions on hypothetical cases from His Majesty's judges, or to shelter departmental decisions or orders against review by the Courts. On the positive side, future legislation would be conducted in such a way as not to repeat these performances. On the negative side, all reasonable steps would be taken to retrace and correct any such errors in the past. It may be said that, in such circumstances, and under such conditions, the mass of fresh legislation would undergo a severe check. Does anybody who has really considered the matter object to that conclusion? The reasonable citizen may well be tempted sometimes to ask the question: For whose benefit and at whose request is this mountain of statutes, and this still greater mountain of rules, orders, and regulations, built up from year to year? The conclusion seems to be unavoidable that the present movement is in a vicious circle. The greater the army of officials, the greater becomes the mass of Parliamentary and departmental legislation; the greater the mass of Parliamentary and departmental legislation, the greater becomes the army of officials; and so on *ad infinitum*. Is not that, at any rate, a mood that would be bridled? What is needed is to re-assert, in grim earnest, the Sovereignty of Parliament and the Rule of Law.

Meantime, it is pertinent to notice, and it may be useful to record, a passage in the speech recently delivered (July 5, 1929) by the Lord Chancellor (Lord Sankey) at the Mansion House. He said that the Rule of Law was the condition of liberty.

> "Amid the cross-currents and shifting sands of public life the Law is like a great rock upon which a man may set his feet and be safe, while the inevitable inequalities of private life are not so dangerous in a country where every citizen knows that in the Law Courts, at any rate, he can get justice. . . . His Majesty's judges are charged with the administration of the law, but there are two matters relating to such administration which in recent years have caused some anxiety not only in the public mind but among trained lawyers. The first is what has been described as a growing tendency to transfer decisions on points of law or fact from the Law Courts to the Minister of some Government department. The second is the general position of the subject when engaged in a dispute with the Crown, or an individual when engaged in a dispute with a department of State. This is neither the time nor the place at which I should pronounce any definite view on either of these points,

but I think that there is a general agreement both within and without the profession that these matters require further careful investigation. And it would be a source of satisfaction to me if it were found possible while I hold office to initiate and complete such an investigation, and to allay the anxiety which no doubt prevails in the public mind with regard to them. Another matter to which public attention should be called is the authority conferred upon a Minister to implement Acts of Parliament by regulation. This is not a modern practice, but one the increase of which in recent years should not be lost sight of."

It might perhaps be well if the amateurs of the new despotism, in their moments of leisure, were to refresh their memories with the opinions which the ancient philosophers so clearly expressed about tyranny. Does anybody suppose that it is any less true to-day than it was in the time of Socrates that despotism is "the worst disorder of a State", or has anybody a real doubt upon the fact that despotism is not only an affront to the citizens, but also an extremely evil thing for the despot himself?

It is sometimes said, but more commonly assumed or implied, that the mischiefs which are here referred to are a necessary consequence of the many-sided activity of Parliament in relation to the life and the fortunes of the individual citizen. The argument, or the suggestion, is that the functions of the State in relation to the individual have gradually come to be so enormously enlarged and intensified in comparison with what they used to be that there is no other way of grappling with the increased volume of legislative business. Parliament, it is said, simply has not time to deal with these matters, and therefore, if they are to be dealt with, the new despotism, however evil, is a necessary evil. It is to be regretted that those who really believe this doctrine do not dare to state it in plain terms. Perhaps one reason why they refrain from that course is that the doctrine, if it were indeed true, might so easily be put the other way round. Where is the arch-defender of bureaucracy who would have the courage to say in the House of Commons: "I am placing these proposals for legislation before the House, but candour compels me to tell the House that the only terms upon which matters so intricate can be disposed of are that my department should be placed above Parliament and beyond the jurisdiction of the Courts?" If, however, that is the real, though unexpressed, belief of the champions of organized lawlessness, it is highly desirable that the public should have a clear view of it. It is right that the public should be made thoroughly well aware of the price which they are invited, or compelled, to pay. If they were really aware of it, they might well think that the price was too high, and that they would prefer to forego the particular commodities which are so expensively to be obtained.

But of course the underlying assumption of the new despotism will not for a moment hold water. Let it be granted, for the sake of the argument, that it is really necessary or desirable for Parliament to exhibit or to attempt the many-sided activity which is put forward as a pretext. Let it be granted, for the sake of the argument, that legislation of the kind would be vastly more cumbrous if recourse were not had to the contrivance of making rules and regulations in matters of detail. Yet the consequences which are here complained of are by no means necessary. Why should the rules and regulations be made behind the back of Parliament? Why, being so made, should they beg the question of *ultra vires* by taking to themselves the force of the statute itself? And why should the whole scheme and system be so contrived as to oust the superintendence and jurisdiction of the Courts? The complaint is not that rules and regulations are made, though they are made, to be sure, in the most embarrassing multiplicity. The complaint is that they are made at such a stage, in such a form, and in such circumstances as to deprive, at one and the same time, both Parliament and the Law Courts of any real authority in relation to them. The citizen is delivered over to the department. The department becomes judge in its own cause. And the measure which produces these results is itself the handiwork of the department. More than that, the method is not occasional nor sporadic. It has become quite systematic. The conclusion is irresistible that it is manifestly the offspring of a well thought out plan, the object and the effect of which are to clothe the department with despotic powers.

Those who favour or defend the accumulation of despotic power in the hands of anonymous officials sometimes suggest the question whether what is really desired by their opponents is that there should be an endless stream of litigation. The question, of course, lacks honesty. It implies, without having the courage to allege, that the aim of the despot in arrogating to himself despotic powers is to save the citizen the burden and the expense of lawsuits. A person who was willing to believe that would be willing to believe anything. No, what is desired is not that there should be endless litigation but rather that litigation should be rendered as a rule unnecessary by the diffused and conscious knowledge that, in case of need, recourse might be had to an impartial public tribunal, governed by precedent, and itself liable to review. Nobody outside Bedlam supposes that the reason why Courts of law exist in a civilized community is that the founders of the State have believed happiness to consist in the greatest possible amount of litigation among the greatest possible number of citizens. The real triumph of Courts of law is when the universal knowledge of their existence, and universal faith in their justice, reduce to a minimum the number of those who are willing so to behave as to expose themselves to their jurisdiction. It is not the individual case that matters. If a person turns any day from the Strand into the Royal Courts of Justice, he may find in one Court a trial about a libel, in another a trial about a partnership, in a third a trial about the sale of goods, and in a fourth (with tolerable certainty) a trial about a collision between two stationary motor-cars. If he thinks of the individual case and the individual case alone, he may hastily conclude that a sad waste of time and of money is going on. But upon further reflection it may occur to him that what is really of value, and of inestimable value, is the public and permanent spectacle which shows that if contracts are broken damages must be paid, if torts are committed unpleasant consequences follow, and if crimes are perpetrated punishment must be suffered; with the total result that in general contracts are not broken, torts are not committed, and crimes are not perpetrated. It is really a vast system of public insurance. The knowledge that the machinery exists, and that when it is employed it is employed with skill and without favour, has the effect of rendering its employment unnecessary save only in the exceptional case.

To apply reflections of this kind to the present matter, it is obvious that the critics of departmental despotism desire, not litigation, but that fairness of decision which, while it renders litigation in general unnecessary, is enormously encouraged and fostered by the prevailing knowledge that, in case of need, there is a Law Court in the background. It is not in the smallest degree desired that the departmental decisions, when they are given, should be of such a kind as to call for review and correction by a Court of law. On the contrary, what is desired is the exact opposite. But the best way of securing that result is to provide that the decision which is taken may, if the party aggrieved be so minded, be brought before the Courts in the ordinary way. Or rather, to be more accurate, it is necessary that there should not be a statutory provision which deprives the aggrieved party of that remedy. The same conclusion is reached if the matter is considered from the point of view not of the citizen but of the department. One has to contemplate a case where some comprehensive scheme or programme is being carried out, under which the rights of particular individuals are, or may be, seriously affected. The statute provides that, if questions of a certain kind arise, the decision is to rest with the Minister—that is, with some official in a particular department. What is likely to be the effect, in the long run, upon the mind of that official if he knows beforehand that any decision which he may give, however unreasonable it may be, and however little capable of being co-ordinated with other decisions given in a similar way, cannot in any circumstances be questioned before a Court? Nobody imagines that he approaches the task with the conscious intention of doing injustice. But it is tolerably obvious that in such a case different considerations may apply from those which would naturally lead up to an extremely careful and well-considered system where every decision was made with the knowledge that at any moment both it and the rest might have to be explained and defended in public before an impartial investigator. Nor should at least two other considerations be overlooked. The first is that, as things stand, the official charged with the final and unimpeachable right of giving the decision is to all intents and purposes the other party to the controversy. The scheme is really ludicrous. One of the parties is absent; there is no hearing; the decision is given by the opposite party; and there is no appeal. It is certainly a simple and expeditious way of disposing of controversial questions. But it is hardly likely to bring into existence a body of case-law that would stand examination. The other consideration—and it is fundamental—is that this invidious task, this almost impossible duty of doubling the parts of suitor and judge in the absence of the other party, is not something which is thrust from outside upon a body of reluctant officials. No, it is they who seek it, it is they who ask for it, and it is they who contrive it. It is not that some other authority shirks and evades the duty. All others are deliberately excluded, and it is a cardinal feature of the departmental scheme, departmentally conceived and departmentally brought to birth, that the department itself should possess these despotic powers. That is a sinister fact which should never be forgotten.

> "Government departments", as Professor Morgan writes in the course of his excellent volume, *Remedies against the Crown*, "are too much inclined to attribute the same sort of mystical efficacy to acts done in virtue of statutory powers as in earlier times they were wont to ascribe to acts invoking the prerogative, and to contend that the mere fact of those acts requiring confirmation by Parliament is sufficient to invest them with a kind of sanctity which puts such acts, even when inchoate, beyond the reach of the law. Where the Courts can intervene, they do so; but the remedy lies to a large extent with public opinion as expressed through its representatives in Parliament. The Parliamentary draftsman's language should be carefully scrutinized by members of Parliament in Committee before they allow legislative measures, delegating large powers to Government departments, to be placed on the Statute Book".

Some highly significant remarks were made at the Royal Academy Banquet, on May 4 1929, by Lord Salisbury, in his reply to the toast of His Majesty's Ministers. He said (see *The Times*, May 6 1929) that—

> "Not merely His Majesty's present Ministers but His Majesty's Government as an institution was the coping-

stone of the Constitution of this country". Nothing, he said, was more clear than that, whatever party was concerned, "the Government was growing in importance every day. The Government was absorbing more and more of the power which used to belong to Parliament. Those who were familiar with public affairs had seen the difficulty under which Parliament itself was conducted, and how the power in the State was concentrated in the Government. In regard to the House of Commons matters had undoubtedly been carried to such a point that complete freedom of speech did not seem to be any longer possible, and a good many details as to important measures could never be discussed there. When they came to the House of Lords, measures reached them so late that there was hardly time to discuss them at all—perhaps just three to four days in which they were called upon to do their duty. Under such circumstances the Government became more and more important, and a greater and greater responsibility rested on it."

A little later, speaking of the enormous increase of a Minister's business during recent years, he said:

"There were memoranda of the Cabinet, there were the memoranda of Committees, and the reports of Committees and of Sub-Committees—papers were mounted higher and higher, so that even if Ministers had nothing else to do it was with the greatest difficulty that they could get through the detailed business, and keep their heads, as it were, above water." Therefore, he concluded, "they could not do better than give their best wishes to the Government, and it did not matter whether the Government of the future was Conservative, Liberal, or Labour—the same sort of difficulties would arise".

The significance of this illuminating passage, it may be suggested, will hardly be impaired if, wherever in it the word "Government" appears, the word "bureaucracy" is substituted for it.

A correspondent of *The Times*, referring recently to "these days when we hear so much of political chiefs as wax in the hands of their permanent officials, and of the ever-increasing power of the bureaucracy", cited a pleasant passage from Plutarch's life of the younger Cato (North's translation). Before taking the office of Quaestor, Cato made particular inquiry what powers attached to it:

> "So he no sooner came to his office, but he presently made great alteration amongst the clerks and officers of the treasury, who, having the laws and records in their hands, and exercising the office commonly under young men which were chosen treasurers (who for their ignorance and lack of experience stood rather in need of ministers to teach them than that they were able to correct others), they themselves were the officers and controlled them. But Cato, not contenting himself with the name and honour of the thing, did thoroughly understand what the clerks and registers should be, and therefore would have them to be, as they ought to be, ministers under the Quaestor only. . . . Thus, having pulled down the pride and stomach of these clerks, and brought them into reason, in short time he had all the tables and records at his commandment, and made the treasure-chamber as honourable as the Senate itself."

The historical parallel may be worth remembering if in

this country zealous officials should ever have the opportunity of congratulating themselves and each other that there is a weak Government in office, and that, therefore, they can do that which seems right in their own eyes. Of all methods of administration that is the worst whereby real power is in the hands of one set of persons while public responsibility belongs to another set of persons. It is a method, as all experience shows, well calculated to encourage the performance of acts which either set of persons, if they had both the responsibility and the power, would be astute to avoid.

In the same context reference may be made to certain remarks of Mr. Justice Eve, in the City of London, on the 17th July 1929 (*The Times*, July 18, 1929).

> "To those" he said, "who were convinced that the best Government was that which governed least, it was alarming to contemplate the increasing scope of legislative interference in those matters which in the past had been considered the private affairs of the citizen. Legislative interference was sometimes supported by attractive pretexts, preceded by certain harmless intrusions, and, if they were tolerated and ignored, the attack would become more aggressive, the advance more permanent and more rapid, and individual liberty and corporate activities would find themselves hampered by unnecessary restraint. The insatiable appetite to control other men's affairs was often evinced by those whose capacity to manage their own affairs was in inverse proportion to their desires."

Nor do the admirers of the new despotism show much appreciation of the actual discouragement and obstacles which its methods so frequently offer to persons engaged in the difficult daily labours of local administration. There is no need to multiply examples. One typical criticism may suffice. At a recent meeting of the Mental Hospitals Association in London, the President, Sir William Hodgson, spoke of the need of a Bill to amend the existing law relating to lunacy.

> "Such a Bill", he said, "would meet with general support if it were formed on enabling rather than compulsory lines, and did not give any powers of larger control to the Central Government department. It was hoped that the new Cabinet would realize that the spirit of local government should be protected from too much arbitrary interference by Government officials, who were apt to be greedy of the power of giving instructions rather than suggestion and information" (*The Times*, July 18, 1929).

A cognate, but quite separate, matter is the important branch of the law which has to do with the position of the Crown as litigant. So long ago as 1921 a Committee, of which the present writer was Chairman, was appointed to consider the matter and to propose such amendments of the law as might be thought "advisable and feasible", due regard being had to the exceptional position of the Crown. In 1924, when various differences had made themselves manifest, and before the drafting of a proposed Bill had been completed, the original terms of reference to the Committee were modified. The Committee was, by the modified reference, requested to prepare a Bill to give effect to certain principles, "on the assumption that the alterations in law involved therein were both desirable and feasible". The Committee was, therefore, relieved—though the fact has perhaps been too little appreciated—of the duty of making any recommendation as to the "desirability or feasibility" of the proposals. Its task became the very different task of drafting a measure which, if it were thought that certain changes could and should be made, might give statutory effect to them. The Report of the Committee, including the text of a draft Bill called the "Crown Proceedings Bill", was presented in February 1927. The chief matters referred to may be described in three propositions, the validity of which was, for the purposes of the Bill, not so much accepted as assumed:

1. That the procedure by Information and Petition of Right should be abolished and the procedure in cases in which the Crown is a litigant should be assimilated, as far as possible, to the procedure regulating the conduct of cases between subjects, including such matters as discovery, the receiving and paying of costs by the Crown, and the like;
2. That the Crown, with certain reservations, should be placed in the same position as a subject as regards the power and liability to sue and be sued in the County Courts; and
3. That the Crown should become liable to be sued in tort.

The draft Bill still remains only a draft Bill. Its merits and demerits do not call for consideration here. But, if and when a serious attempt is made to transfer it to the Statute-Book, some of its provisions will require, and will no doubt receive, careful consideration, including provisions which might have the effect of enabling a Government department to mix itself up in litigation at its own will and pleasure, freed from any check or control on the part of the Law Officers of the Crown or the Treasury solicitor.

CHAPTER IX

SOME LEADING CASES

It seemed convenient, in dealing with the cases mentioned in this chapter, to reproduce the material portions of the judgements as reported in the regular Reports. The reader is in this way enabled to study the views of eminent judges as expressed in their own words.

In *Scott* v. *Scott* the question in issue was whether, in a wife's suit for nullity of marriage, the Court had jurisdiction to order a hearing *in camera*, and the House of Lords decided this question in the negative. The judgements of the Law Lords are important, irrespective of the particular point decided, in that they emphasize the great importance of publicity in the administration of justice. It is laid down that, in contests between parties, secrecy is permissible only in those exceptional cases, such as litigation in reference to a secret process, where publicity would necessarily prevent justice from being done. Mere expediency is not enough to displace the principle that the Courts are bound to administer justice in public. A departure from the principle is permitted only when to apply it would in effect be a denial of justice.

The judgement of Lord Shaw may be thought specially worthy of consideration. He describes publicity in the administration of justice as one of the surest guarantees of our liberties, and a violation of such publicity as an attack upon the very foundations of public and private security, and he cites Bentham:

> "In the darkness of secrecy, sinister interest and evil in every shape have full swing. Only in proportion as publicity has place can any of the checks applicable to judicial injustice speak. Where there is no publicity there is no justice." "Publicity is the very soul of justice. It is the keenest spur to exertion and the surest of all guards against improbity. It keeps the judge himself while trying under trial." "The security of securities is publicity."

In *Local Government Board* v. *Arlidge*, the Board had dismissed an appeal by Arlidge against a refusal by a local authority to determine a closing order under section 17 of the Housing, Town Planning, etc., Act, 1909, and Arlidge applied to the Court for a writ of certiorari to bring up the order dismissing the appeal that it might be quashed on the grounds that the order did not disclose which officer of the Board had decided the appeal, that the applicant had been refused an oral hearing, and that he was not permitted to see the report of the Inspector who held the necessary public inquiry before the appeal was dismissed. The Court of Appeal thought that the principles of natural justice had not been observed, and made absolute a rule for a writ of certiorari. The House of Lords reversed this decision. It was laid down that, where an executive department is entrusted by Parliament with judicial duties, Parliament must, in the absence of an indication to the contrary, be taken to have intended it to follow its own procedure, and though it must act honestly and by honest means, and give to each of the parties the opportunity adequately to present the case made, it was not bound to employ the methods of a Court of Justice. The effect of the decision seems to be that where judicial functions are vested in a Minister or Government department, parties to the proceedings have none of the securities against injustice which they enjoy in judicial proceedings before the Courts.

In *Rex* v. *Halliday* it was held by the House of Lords (Lord Shaw of Dunfermline dissenting) that an order for the internment of a naturalized British subject of German birth, made during the Great War in pursuance of a regulation for securing the public safety and the defence of the realm under the Defence of the Realm Consolidation Act, 1914, was valid. The regulation provided that where, on the recommendation of a competent naval or military authority or of an advisory committee, it appeared to the Secretary of State that, for securing the public safety or the defence of the realm, it was expedient in view of the hostile origin or associations of any person that he should be subject to certain obligations and restrictions, the Secretary of State might by order require that person forthwith to be interned in such place as might be specified in the order, and might be dealt with in like manner as a prisoner of war. There was a proviso that, in the case of any person who was not an enemy subject, the order should include express provision for the due consideration by an advisory committee of any representations he might make against the order. The principal question was whether this regulation was a valid exercise by His Majesty in Council of the power to issue regulations for securing the public safety and the defence of the realm, given by section 1 (1) of the above-mentioned Act.

In the *Institute of Patent Agents* v. *Lockwood*, the question for decision was whether certain rules made by the Board of Trade under the Patents, Designs, and Trade Marks Acts, 1883 and 1888, were *intra* or *ultra vires*. Section 101 (3) of the Act of 1883 provided that the rules, subject to their being laid before both Houses of Parliament, and being liable to annulment on a resolution of either House within forty days after they had been laid before that House, should be of the same effect as if they were contained in the Act and should be judicially noticed. The rules in question had been duly laid before Parliament and had not been objected to within the forty days. It was held by the House of Lords that the rules were *intra vires*. The importance of the case, however, lies in the fact that the Law Lords expressed opinions with regard to the very important question whether, in view of the provision that the rules should be of the same effect as if they were contained in the Act, it was open to the Courts to canvass their validity. The point was not decided, because, the rules having been held to be *intra vires*, it became unnecessary to give a decision upon it. The Lord Chancellor (Lord Herschell) and Lords Watson and Russell of Killowen thought that it was not competent for the Courts to question the validity of the rules, but Lord Morris was of a contrary opinion. The Lord Chancellor thought that the words "shall be of the same effect as if they were contained in this Act" were really meaningless unless they meant that for all purposes of construction or obligation, or otherwise, the rules were to be treated exactly as if they were in the Act. Lord Morris thought that the only rules which were to have statutory effect were rules such as the Legislature had delegated to the Board of Trade the authority of making, and that it was the duty of the Court to decide whether rules which were challenged as being *ultra vires* were within the power delegated to the Board of Trade.

In *Chester* v. *Bateson* the question was whether a certain regulation purporting to be made under section 1 of the Defence of the Realm Consolidation Act, 1914, giving power to His Majesty in Council to issue regulations for securing the public safety and the defence of the realm, was valid. The regulation in question provided that if, as respects any area in which work on war material was being carried on, the Minister of Munitions was of opinion that the ejectment from their dwellings of workmen employed in that work was calculated to impede, delay, or restrict that work, he might by order declare the area to be a special area, and that, whilst the order remained in force, no person should, without his consent, take any proceedings for the ejectment of a tenant of any dwelling-house or other premises situate in the special area, being a house or premises in which any workman so employed was living, so long as the tenant continued duly to pay the rent and observe the other conditions of the tenancy. It was declared that any person contravening the regulation should be guilty of a summary offence. It was held that the regulation was *ultra vires*. The prevention of the disturbance of munition workers in their dwellings was in itself reasonable, but this object could have been attained by providing that no order for ejectment should be made except under prescribed conditions. It was not a necessary, nor even a reasonable, way to aid in securing the public safety and the defence of the realm to deprive the King's subjects of their right of access to the Courts of Justice unless with the permission of a Minister.

R. v. *Home Secretary, ex parte O'Brien*, was an application for a writ of *habeas corpus* directed to the Home Secretary. By a regulation made under the Restoration of Order in Ireland Act, 1920, which empowered His Majesty in Council to issue regulations for securing the restoration of order in Ireland, it was provided that where, on the recommendation of a competent naval or military authority or of an advisory committee, it appeared to the Secretary of State that, for securing the restoration or maintenance of order in Ireland, it was expedient that a person who was suspected of acting in a manner prejudicial to that object should be subjected to restrictions, the Secretary of State might by order require that person to be interned in any place in the British Islands. On December 5, 1922, the Irish Free State Constitution Act, giving the Irish Free State a separate executive, was passed. On March 7, 1923, the Home Secretary made an order under the regulation that Mr. O'Brien, who then resided in England, should be interned in the Irish Free State in such place as might be determined by the Irish Free State Government. The Free State Government agreed with the Home Secretary that, if an advisory committee should decide that Mr. O'Brien ought not to have been deported, he must be released. It was held by the Court of Appeal that the regulation in question was impliedly repealed by the Irish Free State Constitution Act, and the order for internment was therefore illegal, and that, in view of the agreement between the Home Secretary and the Irish Free State Government, a writ of habeas corpus ought to issue addressed to the Home Secretary. Lord Justice Bankes, at the conclusion of his judgement, commented on the inconvenience and dangers incident to legislation by Order in Council. The case is a striking example of the application of the "rule of law" in aid of the liberty of the subject.

In *R.* v. *Electricity Commissioners* the Commissioners had formulated a scheme for the improvement of the organization for the supply of electricity in a certain district, in purported exercise of their powers under sections 5 and 6 of the Electricity (Supply) Act, 1919, and were proceeding to hold a local inquiry on the scheme as required by the Act. By section 7 (1) of the Act the Commissioners may make an order giving effect to a scheme embodying decisions arrived at as the result of the local inquiry, and present the order for confirmation by the Minister of Transport, who may confirm it with or without modification as he thinks fit; and by section 7 (2) any order so confirmed is to be laid before Parliament, and is not to come into operation until it has been approved, with or without modification, by a resolution passed by each House, and when so approved it "shall have effect as if enacted in this Act". On an application for writs of prohibition and certiorari, it was held by the Court of Appeal that, the scheme being *ultra vires*, a writ of prohibition should issue, prohibiting the Commissioners from proceeding further with the consideration of the scheme. The case is important as showing that the Court is not precluded by this form of legislation from intervening if the Government department exceeds the limits of its authority. Lord Justice Younger (as he then was) seemed to be of opinion that, even if an order had been confirmed by the Minister of Transport and approved by resolution of both Houses, it would still have been open to the Court to inquire whether the scheme was one which under the Act the Commissioners had power to formulate, and, if not, to quash the order as *ultra vires*. This view is in accordance with the dissenting view of Lord Morris in the *Institute of Patent Agents* v. *Lockwood*.

In the *Board of Education* v. *Rice* the Board had purported to decide certain questions submitted to them for decision under section 7 (3) of the Education Act, 1902. It was laid down that in deciding such questions the Board were in the nature of an arbitral tribunal, from whose determination in law or fact there was no appeal to a Court of Law, provided that they acted in good faith and fairly listened to both sides. But, as the Board had not in the particular case determined the questions submitted to them, it was held that the purported decision must be brought up by certiorari and quashed, and that a writ of mandamus must issue commanding the Board to determine the questions.

SCOTT *v.* SCOTT, L.R. (1913), Appeal Cases, 417

A wife's suit for nullity of marriage on the ground of her husband's impotence was ordered by the Probate, Divorce, and Admiralty Division to be heard *in camera*, and the petitioner, after a decree *nisi* had been pronounced, published to certain persons copies of the shorthand writer's notes of the proceedings. This publication having been held to be a contempt of Court, it was decided, on an appeal to the House of Lords, that the Court had no jurisdiction to make the order for a hearing *in camera.*

(P. 437) The LORD CHANCELLOR (Viscount Haldane): While the broad principle is that the Courts of this country must, as between parties, administer justice in public, this principle is subject to apparent exceptions. . . . But the exceptions are themselves the outcome of a yet more fundamental principle that the chief object of Courts of Justice must be to secure that justice is done. In the two cases of wards of Courts and of lunatics, the Court is really sitting primarily to guard the interests of the ward or the lunatic. Its jurisdiction is in this respect parental and administrative, and the disposal of controverted questions is an incident only in the jurisdiction. It may often be necessary, in order to attain its primary object, that the Court should exclude the public. The broad principle which ordinarily governs it therefore yields to the paramount duty, which is the care of the ward or the lunatic. The other case referred to, that of litigation as to secret process, where the effect of publicity would be to destroy the subject-matter, illustrates a class which stands on a different footing. There it may well be that justice could not be done at all if it had to be done in public. As the paramount object must always be to do justice, the general rule as to publicity, after all only the means to an end, must accordingly yield. But the burden lies on those seeking to displace (p. 438) its application in the particular case to make out that the ordinary rule must as of necessity be superseded by this paramount consideration. The question is by no means one which, consistently with the spirit of our jurisprudence, can be dealt with by the judge as resting in his mere discretion as to what is expedient. The latter must treat it as one of principle, and as turning, not on convenience, but on necessity. . . . Unless it be strictly necessary for the attainment of justice, there can be no power in the Court to hear *in camera* either a matrimonial cause or any other where there is a contest between parties. He who maintains that by no other means than by such a hearing can justice be done may apply for an unusual procedure. But he must make out his case strictly, and bring it up to the standard which the underlying principle requires. . . . He must satisfy the Court that by nothing short of the exclusion of the public can justice be done. . . .

(P. 440) EARL OF HALSBURY: . . . I am of opinion that every Court of Justice is open to every subject of the King. I will deal presently with what have been called exceptions to that rule, though I think it is a mistake as to some of the so-called exceptions thus to describe them, but I want in the first instance to emphasize the broad rule I believe to be the law.

I believe this has been the rule, at all events, for some

centuries, but, as I will attempt to show presently, it has been the unquestioned rule since 1857, unquestioned by anything that I can recognize as an authority.

. . . . . .

(P. 441). There are three different exceptions commonly so called, though in my judgement two of them are no exceptions at all. The first is wardship and the relation between guardian and ward, and the second is the care and treatment of lunatics.

My Lords, neither of these, for a reason that hardly (p. 442) requires to be stated, forms part of the public administration of justice at all.

Again, the acceptance of the aid of a judge as arbitrator to deal with private family disputes has, by the express nature of it, no relation to the public administration of justice. . . .

My Lords, while I agree with the Lord Chancellor in the result which he has arrived at in this case, and generally in the principles he has laid down, I wish to guard myself against the proposition that a judge may bring a case within the category of enforced secrecy because he thinks that justice cannot be done unless it is heard in secret. I do not deny it, because it is impossible to prove what cases might or might not be brought within that category, but I should require to have brought before me the concrete case before I could express an opinion upon it. . . .

(P. 445). EARL LOREBURN: . . . I cannot think that the High Court has an unqualified power in its discretion to hear civil proceedings with closed doors. The inveterate rule is that justice shall be administered in open Court. I do not speak of the parental jurisdiction regarding lunatics or wards of Court, or of what may be done in chambers, which is a distinct and by no means short subject, or of special statutory restrictions. I speak of the trial of actions, including petitions for divorce or nullity, in the High Court. To this rule of publicity there are exceptions, and we must see whether any principle can be deduced from the cases in which the exception has been allowed.

It has been held that when the subject-matter of the action would be destroyed by a hearing in open Court, as in a case of some secret process of manufacture, the doors may be closed. I think this may be justified upon wider ground. Farwell, L.J., aptly cites Lord Eldon as saying, in a case of quite a different kind, that he dispensed with the presence of some of the parties "in order to do all that can be done for the purpose of justice rather than hold that no justice shall subsist among persons who may have entered into these contracts". An aggrieved person, entitled to protection against one man who had stolen his secret, would not ask for it on the terms that the secret was to be communicated to all the world. There would be in effect a denial of justice.

Again, the Court may be closed or cleared if such a precaution is necessary for the administration of justice. (P. 446) Tumult or disorder, or the just apprehension of it, would certainly justify the exclusion of all from whom such interruption is expected, and, if discrimination is impracticable, the exclusion of the public in general. Or witnesses may be ordered to withdraw, lest they trim their evidence by hearing the evidence of others. Or, to use the language of Fletcher Moulton, L.J., in very exceptional cases . . . where a judge finds that a portion of the trial is rendered impracticable by the presence of the public, he may exclude them so far as to enable the trial to proceed. It would be impossible to enumerate or anticipate all possible contingencies, but in all cases where the public has been excluded with admitted propriety, the underlying principle, as it seems to me, is that the administration of justice would be rendered impracticable by their presence, whether because the case could not be effectively tried, or the parties entitled to justice would be reasonably deterred from seeking it at the hands of the Court.

(P. 447) . . . Some passages in various judgements in this and other cases indicate that the Court has a right to close its doors in the interest of public decency. Apart from some Act of Parliament authorizing such a course in particular cases, I regret that I cannot find warrant for this opinion. However true it may be that the publicity given to obscene or bestial matter by trial in open Court stimulates and suggests imitation, as many judges have learnt from experience at assizes, and however deplorable it may be that they have no power to prevent it, the remedy must be found by the Legislature or not at all. It is a great evil. And though the traditional law, that English justice must be administered openly in the face of all men, is an almost priceless inheritance, it does seem strange that it may be relaxed in order to save property, but cannot be relaxed in order to safeguard public decency against even the foules contamination. . . .

(P. 463) Lord Atkinson: . . . The hearing of a case in public may be, and often is, no doubt, painful, humiliating, or deterrent both to parties and witnesses, and in many cases, especially those of a criminal nature, the details may be so indecent as to tend to injure public morals, but all this is tolerated and endured, because it is felt that in public trial is to be found, on the whole, the best security for the pure, impartial, and efficient administration of justice, the best means for winning for it public confidence and respect. . . .

(P. 476) Lord Shaw of Dunfermline: . . . I am of opinion that the order to hear this case *in camera* was beyond the power of the judge to pronounce. I am further of opinion that, even on the assumption that such an order had been within his power, it was beyond his power to impose a suppression of all reports of what had passed at the trial after the trial had come to an end. So taken, my Lords, they appear to me to constitute a violation of that publicity in the administration of justice which is one of the surest guarantees of our liberties, and an attack upon the very foundations of public and private security.

. . . I admit the embarrassment produced to the learned judge of first instance and to the majority of the Court of Appeal by the state of the decisions; but those decisions, in my humble judgement, or rather—for it is in nearly all the instances only so—these expressions of opinion by the way, have signified not only an encroachment upon and suppression of private right, but the gradual invasion and undermining of constitutional security. This result, which is declared by the Courts below to have been legitimately

(p. 477) reached under a free Constitution, is exactly the same result which would have been achieved under, and have accorded with, the genius and practice of despotism. What has happened is a usurpation—a usurpation which could not have been allowed even as a prerogative of the Crown, and most certainly must be denied to the judges of the land. To remit the maintenance of constitutional rights to the region of judicial discretion is to shift the foundations of freedom from the rock to the sand.

It is needless to quote authority on this topic from legal, philosophical, or historical writers. It moves Bentham over and over again. "In the darkness of secrecy sinister interest and evil in every shape have full swing. Only in proportion as publicity has place can any of the checks applicable to judicial injustice operate. Where there is no publicity there is no justice." "Publicity is the very soul of justice. It is the keenest spur to exertion and the surest of all guards against improbity. It keeps the judge himself while trying under trial." "The security of securities is publicity." But amongst historians the grave and enlightened verdict of Hallam, in which he ranks the publicity of judicial proceedings even higher than the rights of Parliament as a guarantee of public security, is not likely to be forgotten: "Civil liberty in this kingdom has two direct guarantees: the open administration of justice according to known laws truly interpreted, and fair constructions of evidence; and the right of Parliament, without let or interruption, to inquire into, and obtain redress of, public grievances. Of these, the first is by far the most indispensable, nor can the subjects of any State be reckoned to enjoy a real freedom where this condition is not found both in its judicial institutions and in their constant exercise."

I myself should be very slow indeed . . . to throw any doubt upon this topic. The right of the citizen and the working of the Constitution in the sense which I have described have upon the whole since the fall of the Stuart dynasty received from the judiciary—and they appear to me still to demand of it—a constant and most watchful respect. There is no greater danger of usurpation than that which proceeds little by little, under cover of rules of (p. 478) procedure, and at the instance of the judges themselves. I must say frankly that I think these encroachments have taken place by way of judicial procedure in such a way as, insensibly at first, but now culminating in this decision most sensibly, to impair the rights, safety, and freedom of the citizen and the open administration of the law.

LOCAL GOVERNMENT BOARD *v.* ARLIDGE, L.R. (1915), Appeal Cases, 120

The Court of Appeal had ordered a writ of certiorari to issue to bring into Court to be quashed an order of the Local Government Board dismissing an appeal of the respondent against a refusal by a local authority to determine a closing order under section 17 of the Housing, Town Planning, etc., Act, 1909. In an appeal to the House of Lords by the Local Government Board, the order of the Court of Appeal was reversed. The grounds upon which the writ of certiorari was applied for were (1) that the order did not disclose by which officer of the Board the appeal had been decided; (2) that the respondent was refused an oral hearing, and (3) that he was not permitted to see the report of the inspector of the Board who held, as required by the statute, a public local inquiry before the appeal was dismissed.

(P. 125) The Lord Chancellor (Viscount Haldane): My Lords, the question which has to be decided in this case is whether the appellants, the Local Government Board, have validly dealt with an appeal brought before them under the provisions of s. 17 of the Housing and Town Planning Act, 1909. The respondent is the assignee of a lease of a dwelling-house, No. 83 Palmerston Road, in the metropolitan borough of Hampstead. On January 12, 1911, the borough council made an order under s. 17, sub-s. 2, of the Act to which I have referred, prohibiting the use of the house for habitation until in their judgement it had been rendered fit for that purpose. On March 7, 1911, the respondent gave notice of appeal to the Local Government Board. That Board intimated, in accordance with s. 39 of the Act and with the rules which it had made thereunder, that it would not decide the appeal without having held a local inquiry. A public inquiry was, as the result, held on May 24, 1911, before Mr. Edward Leonard, one of the housing inspectors of the Board designated for that purpose, who also made a personal inspection of the house on June 2 following. . . . On June 6 the inspector submitted to the Board his report of the inspection, and on July 29, 1911, the Board, after considering the report and the other documents before them, confirmed the closing order. . . .

(P. 127) (Subsequently) the respondent applied to the borough council to determine the closing order having regard to the repairs which he had effected, and on October 5, 1911, the council refused on the ground that the premises had not been rendered fit for habitation. On October 19 the respondent appealed again to the Board, this time against the refusal to determine the closing order. . . . On November 25, 1911, the Board gave notice to the respondent of their intention to hold a second public local inquiry with respect to his appeal against the refusal of the borough council to determine the closing order. The inquiry was held on December 8 before the same inspector. The respondent was present with his solicitor and witnesses, and the borough council and the London County Council were also represented. The respondent's solicitor argued his case, and the respondent and his witnesses gave evidence. On December 13 the inspector submitted to the Board his report, together with a shorthand note of the evidence and speeches. On January 8, 1912, the Board intimated to the respondent that it would be willing to consider any further statement in writing which he desired to submit to it. The respondent did not avail himself of this opportunity, but applied for writ of certiorari to remove the order of the Board into the King's Bench Division to be quashed, on the ground that the appeal had been determined in the manner provided by the law. The points taken were that the appeal had been decided neither by the Board nor by anyone lawfully authorized to act for them, and that the procedure adopted by the Board was contrary to natural justice in that the respondent had not been afforded an opportunity of being heard orally before the Board. I assume further, what appears to have been the case, that the point was also taken that the report of the inspector on the second inquiry was not disclosed to the respondent. This point was certainly afterwards argued in the Court of Appeal.

(P. 128) . . . The learned judges of the King's Bench Division declined to hold that the appeal had not been properly disposed of, both in form and substance. . . .

The Court of Appeal, consisting of Vaughan Williams, Buckley, and Hamilton, L.JJ., by a majority took a different view and reversed the decision. Vaughan Williams, L.J., held that the appeal was one *inter partes*, the respondent and the Hampstead Local Board being the opposing parties. He thought that the duty of the Board was to hear both sides, and to disclose all the evidence of fact laid before them, and the conclusions of law adopted by them as the basis of their decision. He held that the non-production to the respondent of the inspector's reports was contrary to the principles of natural justice, and that, in the absence of a plain direction in the statute abrogating the necessity of observing these principles in dealing with the reports, the principles of English justice had been (p. 129) violated. He appeared further to think that the absence of any statement by or on behalt of the Board as to which of its members considered the appeal was a further objection to the validity of the Board's order.

Buckley, L.J., thought the importance of the general question which was raised very great. It was increasingly common for statutes to empower Government departments to decide questions affecting rights of property, and it was of the first importance that their proceedings should be so conducted as to command the confidence of the public, and that the principles applicable to their conduct should be well understood. A mere power to make rules determining the procedure in such appeals did not obviate the necessity of such rules being in accordance with natural justice. It was essential that each of the parties should know the case the other made and should be heard in the other's presence. Assuming that it could be validly proved that the original hearing should assume the form of a statement in writing, it was not clear that a party who subsequently desired to be heard orally could be debarred from claiming to be so heard.

The learned Lord Justice thought that as the local authority was the authority against which the appeal to the Board was brought, it was in one sense not a party litigant, but, as it could be ordered to make a counter-statement and to pay or receive costs, for all material purposes it was not to be distinguished from a party litigant, and therefore the other party ought to know the case it made. Having regard to the terms of s. 5 of 34 & 35 Vict. c. 70, which constituted the Board and provided that anything to be done on its behalf might be done by the President or any member, or by a secretary or assistant secretary authorized by its General Order, the inspector was not within the class of persons who could decide anything. If he made a report on a public inquiry held by him it should be made public. A case could not be argued before one man and decided by another. The respondent had, therefore, no real opportunity of presenting his case when he was invited by the letter of January 8, 1912, to do so, for he was not permitted to see the report.

(P. 130) Hamilton, L.J., was of a different opinion. The practice, he said, of the Board, like that of its predecessor the Poor Law Board, had always been to dispose by correspondence of appeals even in important matters such as an auditor's disallowance of items, and in treating the inspector's report as confidential it was only following an old and well-known practice. The question was whether, if the statute itself did not in terms authorize the practice, it was contrary to natural justice, "an expression sadly lacking in precision". He referred to several precedents, and came to the conclusion that it was a sound inference, to be drawn, as matter of construction, that the Legislature, aware, as he took it to have been, of the practice as to these inquiries and its incidents, intended that the local inquiry which it prescribed should be the usual local inquiry, and that the usual incidents should attach in default of any special enactment, including the incident that the Board should treat the report as confidential. He was of opinion that what had been done was in accordance with the Act of 1909.

My Lords, I have thought it important to set out with some fullness the conflicting views in the Court of Appeal. It is obvious that two of the judges there based their conclusions on the principle that in the absence of a direction to the contrary, which they could not find in the statute, the analogy of the procedure in a Court of Justice must guide them. Hamilton, L.J., on the contrary, thought that he found in the statute a scheme of procedure that excluded this analogy. Which of these opinions was right can only be determined by referring to the language of the Legislature. Here, as in other cases, we have simply to construe that language and to abstain from guessing at what Parliament had in its mind, except in so far as the language enables us to do so. There is no doubt that the question is one affecting property and the liberty of a man to do what he chooses with what is his own. Such rights are not to be affected unless Parliament has said so. But Parliament, in what it considers higher interests than those of the individual, has so often interfered with such rights on other occasions, that it is dangerous for judges to lay much stress on what a hundred years ago would have been (p. 131) a presumption considerably stronger than it is to-day.

(P. 132) . . . My Lords, when the duty of deciding an appeal is imposed, those whose duty it is to decide it must act judicially. They must deal with the question referred to them without bias, and they must give to each of the parties the opportunity of adequately presenting the case made. The decision must be come to in the spirit and with the sense of responsibility of a tribunal whose duty it is to mete out justice. But it does not follow that the procedure of every such tribunal must be the same. In the case of a Court of Law, tradition in this country has prescribed certain principles to which in the main the procedure must conform. But what that procedure is to be in detail must depend on the nature of the tribunal. In modern times it has become increasingly common for Parliament to give an appeal in matters which really pertain to administration, rather than to the exercise of judicial functions of an ordinary Court, to authorities whose functions are administrative and not in the ordinary sense judicial. Such a body as the Local Government Board has the duty of enforcing obligations on the individual which are imposed in the interests of the community. Its character is that of an organization with executive functions. In that it resembles other great departments of the State. When, therefore, Parliament entrusts it with judicial duties, Parliament must be taken, in the absence of any declaration to the contrary, to have intended it to follow the procedure which is its own, and is necessary if it is to be capable of doing its work efficiently. . . .

(P. 133) . . . In the case of the Local Government Board it is not doubtful what this procedure is. The Minister at the head of the Board is directly responsible to Parliament like other Ministers. He is responsible not only for what he himself does, but for all that is done in his department. The volume of work entrusted to him is very great and he cannot do the bulk of it himself. He is expected to obtain his materials vicariously through his officials, and he has discharged his duty if he sees that they obtain these materials for him properly. . . . Unlike a judge in a Court he is not only at liberty but is compelled to rely on the assistance of his staff. When, therefore, the Board is directed to dispose of an appeal, that does not mean that any particular official of the Board is to dispose of it. . . . It is said that the report (p. 134) of the inspector should have been disclosed. It might or might not have been useful to disclose this report, but I do not think that the Board was bound to do so, any more than it would have been bound to disclose all the minutes made on the papers in the office before a decision was come to. . . . I do not think the Board was bound to hear the respondent orally, provided it gave him the opportunities he actually had. Moreover, I doubt whether it is correct to speak of the case as a *lis inter partes*. The Hampstead Borough Council was itself acting administratively, although it had the right to appear, and did appear, before the inspector and on the appeal, and might have to pay or receive costs. . . .

(P. 136) LORD SHAW OF DUNFERMLINE: . . . It is said that the respondent is entitled to know his particular judge or judges, to individualize the Board, and to demand that that person or those persons so discovered shall give him, the respondent, an audience on the whole material available, including the result of the public local inquiry and the report made thereupon by the Board's inspector. In the first place, of the demand to know the individual judge or judges. My Lords, how can the judiciary be blind to the well-known facts applicable not only to the constitution but to the working of such branches of the Executive? The department is represented in Parliament by its responsible head. . . . His Board—that is, all the members of it together—may never meet, or they may only be convened on some question of policy; but a determination, signed and sealed and issued in correct form, stands as the deliverance of the Board as such, for which determination the President becomes answerable to Parliament. . . .

. . . The next proposition is this, that when a public local inquiry has been held in compliance with statute, the person whose interests are affected is entitled to something more, namely, a disclosure of the views of the inspector written out by him, in jottings or otherwise, for the guidance or consideration of the department in dealing with the case.

(P. 137) . . . I incline to hold that the disadvantage in very many cases would exceed the advantage of such disclosure. And I feel certain that if it were laid down in Courts of Law that such disclosure could be compelled, a serious impediment might be placed upon that frankness which ought to obtain among a staff accustomed to elaborately detailed and often most delicate and difficult tasks. . . .

(P. 138) The words "natural justice" occur in arguments and sometimes in judicial pronouncements in such cases. My Lords, when a central administrative board deals with an appeal from a local authority it must do its best to act justly, and to reach just ends by just means. If a statute prescribes the means, it must employ them. If it is left without express guidance, it must still act honestly and by honest means. In regard to these, certain ways and methods of judicial procedure may very likely be imitated; and lawyer-like methods may find especial favour from lawyers. But that the judiciary should presume to impose its own methods on administrative or executive officers is a usurpation. And the assumption that the methods of natural justice are *ex necessitate* those of Courts of Justice is wholly unfounded. . . .

(P. 146) Lord Moulton: . . . I have no doubt that the new procedure as to appeal was intended to be an appeal to a superior executive body as such, and that it was not intended that the Local Government Board should act in a purely judicial capacity. There is no doubt that it must act "in a judicial temper". Its order might confirm an order of the local authority interfering with the property (p. 147) of a private individual, and thereupon that order would be capable of legal enforcement. In the exercise of such powers the Local Government Board would be bound to treat the matter in a judicial spirit, availing itself of the wide powers solely for the purpose of carrying into effect in the best way the provisions of the Act. But although in this sense it must act judicially, there was not, in my opinion, any obligation upon it to follow wholly, or in any special respects, the procedure of a Court of Justice, provided that the procedure adopted by them was consistent with their performance of their duties judicially in the sense to which I have referred.

(P. 151) . . . There is one point which needs notice, namely, the claim that the respondent was entitled as of right to see the report of the inspector who held the public inquiry.

No such right is given by statute or by an established custom of the department. Like every administrative body, the Local Government Board must derive its knowledge from its agents, and I am unable to see any reason why the reports which they make to the department should be made public. It would, in my opinion, cripple the usefulness of these inquiries. It is not for me to express my opinion as to the desirability of an administrative department taking any particular course in such matters, but I entirely dissociate myself from the remarks which have been made in this case in favour of a department making reports of this kind public. Such a practice would, in my opinion, be decidedly mischievous.

REX *v.* HALLIDAY, L.R. (1917), Appeal Cases, 260

Held, by the Lord Chancellor (Lord Finlay), and Lords Dunedin, Atkinson, and Wrenbury, Lord Shaw of Dunfermline dissenting, that an order for the internment of a naturalized British subject of German birth, made during the Great War in pursuance of a Regulation for securing the public safety and the defence of the realm under the Defence of the Realm Consolidation Act, 1914, was valid.

(P. 264) The LORD CHANCELLOR (Lord Finlay): My Lords, the appellant in this case is a naturalized British subject of German birth who has been interned by an order made by the Secretary of State under the powers of Reg. 14B, which was made under the Defence of the Realm Consolidation Act, 1914.

It was contended on behalf of the appellant that Reg. 14B was not authorized by the Act and was *ultra vires*.

It is beyond all dispute that Parliament has power to authorize the making of such a regulation. The only question is whether on a true construction of the Act it has done so. (After setting out the provisions of s. 1, sub-s. 1, of the Act, and of Reg. 14B of the Defence of the Realm (p. 266) (Consolidated) Regulations, his Lordship proceeded.) It will be observed that any action of the Secretary of State under this regulation is to be upon the recommendation of a competent naval or military authority or of an advisory committee. If on such recommendation it appears to the Secretary of State that, for securing the public safety or defence of the realm, it is expedient so to do, he may subject any person of hostile origin or associations to (p. 267) certain restrictions, one of which is internment. The order must, however, include provision in the case of any person not being an enemy subject for consideration of any representation which the person affected may make against the order by an advisory committee, which is to be presided over by a person who holds or has held high judicial office. The regulation, therefore, provides means for ascertaining whether any complaint against the justice or necessity of the order is well founded.

(P. 268) . . . It was contended (1) that some limitation must be put upon the general words of the statute; (2) that there is no provision for imprisonment without trial; (3) that the provisions made by the Defence of the Realm Act, 1915, for the trial of British subjects by a civil Court with a jury strengthened the contention of the appellant; (4) that general words in a statute could not take away the vested rights of the subject or alter the fundamental law of the Constitution; (5) that the statute is in its nature penal and must be strictly construed; (6) that a construction said to be repugnant to the constitutional traditions of this country could not be adopted.

Reference was made by the appellant's counsel to the history of the various interferences with a right to habeas corpus in times of public danger, and it was urged that if it had been intended to interfere with personal liberty this is the course which would have been adopted.

I am unable to accede to any of the arguments urged on behalf of the appellant.

It was not, as I understand the argument, contended that the words of the statute are not in their natural meaning wide enough to authorize such a regulation as Reg. 14B, but it was strongly contended that some limitation must be put upon these words, as an unrestricted interpretation might involve extreme consequences, such as, it was suggested, the infliction of the punishment of death without trial.

It appears to me to be a sufficient answer to this argument that it may be necessary in a time of great public (p. 269) danger to entrust great powers to His Majesty in Council, and that Parliament may do so feeling certain that such powers will be reasonably exercised. . . .

(P. 270) The statute was passed at a time of supreme national danger, which still exists. The danger of espionage and of damage by secret agents to ships, railways, munition works, bridges, etc., had to be guarded against. The restraint imposed may be a necessary measure of precaution, and in the interests of the whole nation it may be regarded as expedient that such an order should be made in suitable cases. This appears to me to be the meaning of the statute. Every reasonable precaution to obviate hardship which is consistent with the object of the regulation appears to have been taken.

It was argued that if the Legislature had intended to interfere with personal liberty it would have provided, as on previous occasions of national danger, for suspension of the rights of the subject as to a writ of habeas corpus. The answer is simple. The Legislature has selected another way of achieving the same purposes, probably milder as well as more effectual than those adopted on the occasion of previous wars.

The suggested rule as to construing penal statutes and the provision as to trial of British subjects by jury made by the Defence of the Realm Act, 1915, have no relevance in dealing with an executive measure by way of preventing a public danger.

LORD DUNEDIN: . . . It is pointed out that the powers, if interpreted as the unanimous judgement of the Courts below interprets them, are drastic and might be abused. That is true. But the fault, if fault there be, lies in the fact that the British Constitution has entrusted to the two Houses of Parliament, subject to the assent of the King, an absolute power untrammelled by any written instrument, (p. 271) obedience to which may be compelled by some judicial body. The danger of abuse is theoretically present; practically, as things exists, it is in my opinion absent. . . .

(P. 276) LORD SHAW OF DUNFERMLINE: . . . I am of opinion that the judgements appealed from are erroneous in law, and that they constitute a suspension and a breach of those fundamental constitutional rights which are protective of British liberty.

The appellant is a naturalized citizen of this country. That is to say, on the one hand he owes submission to, and on the other he is entitled to the protection of, our laws. That is the essential pact underlying naturalization. The War made no difference to this. . . .

(P. 277) I am clearly of opinion that, although bearing to

be a regulation, this is, in truth and essentially, not a regulation at all, and that it was *ultra vires* of His Majesty in Council to issue under the guise of a regulation an authorization for the apprehension, seizure, and internment without trial of any of the lieges. In my view, Parliament never sanctioned, either in intention or by reason of the statutory words employed in the Defence of the Realm Acts, such a violent exercise of arbitrary power. It follows that the order or fiat of the Secretary of State which has already been quoted is also *ultra vires*. . . .

(P. 278) My Lords, the Act of Parliament, as we shall see, does employ the words "for securing the public safety and the defence of the realm", but there is not one word in the Act of Parliament about "hostile origin or associations" of any person, nor indeed about internment.

These are not statutory terms. Parliament might very well have taken the subject of "hostile origin or associations" into its account; and Parliament might very well have considered the subject of internment and dealt with it. Had it done so, Courts of Law would have been bound to comply with any verdict on the subject which it embodied in statute.

Accordingly the first great and broad fact confronting your Lordships in this case is that in a matter so fundamentally affecting the rights of His Majesty's subjects Parliament has given no express sanction for the introduction of that language "hostile origin or associations". And what remains is the argument that Parliament, not expressly dealing with a matter pre-eminently demanding careful delimitation, must be held to have accomplished by implication this far-reaching subversion of our liberties.

To this argument I am respectfully unable to accede. I do not think that the Defence of the Realm Acts can be submitted to such a violent and strained construction. . . .

(P. 285) . . . The words, it is said, are perfectly general; the King in Council is vested with powers to judge of what is for the public safety and the defence of the realm, and to act accordingly. All the rest of those statutes as to trial, intimation, notification of rights; every provision for the legal disposal of the question affecting liberty—all this is on one side, the side of offence against a regulation; on the other side stands this super-eminent power of the Government of the day. In the exercise of that power the plainest teachings of history and dictates of justice demand that, on the one hand, Government power, and, on the other, individual rights—these two—shall face each other as party and party. But it is not so, so it is said: here the Government as a party shall act at its own hand; the subject as a party shall submit and shall not be heard; the Government is at once to be party, judge, and executioner. When—so is the logic of the argument—Parliament took elaborate pains to make a legal course and legal remedy plain to the subject as to all the regulations which were stated in detail, there was one thing which Parliament did not disclose, but left Courts of Law to imply—namely, that Parliament, all the time and intentionally, left another deadly weapon in the hands of the Government of the day under which the remainder of those very Acts, not to speak of the entire body of the laws of these islands protective of liberty, would be avoided. As occasion served the Government of the day, despotic force could be wielded, and that whole fabric of protection be gone. My Lords, I do not believe Parliament intended anything of the kind. . . .

(P. 307) LORD WRENBURY: . . . There is room for difference of opinion whether what I may call legislation by devolution is expedient; whether a statute ought not to be self-contained; whether it is desirable that a statute should provide that regulations made by a defined authority or in a defined matter shall themselves have the effect of a statute. But I think it clear that this statute has conferred upon His Majesty in Council power to issue regulations which, when issued, will take effect as if they were contained in the statute.

. . . No doubt every statutory authority must be exercised honestly. There is, I conceive, no other limit upon the acts that the regulations may authorize to achieve the defined object.

INSTITUTE OF PATENT AGENTS *v.* LOCKWOOD, L.R. (1894), Appeal Cases, 347

By section 101 of the Patents, Designs and Trade Marks Act, 1883, the Board of Trade were given power to make such general rules as they thought expedient, subject to the provisions of the Act, for regulating the practice of registration under the Act. Sub.-s. (3) provided that rules made in pursuance of the section should (subject as thereinafter mentioned) be of the same effect as if they were contained in the Act, and should be judicially noticed, and sub.-s. (4) that any rules made should be laid before both Houses of Parliament and should be advertised. Sub.-s. (5) provided that if either House, within forty days after any rules had been so laid before the House, resolve that such rules or any of them ought to be annulled, the same should after the date of such resolution be of no effect. By section 1, sub.-s. (2) of the Patents, Designs and Trade Marks Act, 1888, a further power was given to the Board of Trade to make general rules for the purposes of that section, and it was declared that the provisions of section 101 of the Act of 1883 should apply to all rules so made as if they were made in pursuance of the said section 101.

The Board of Trade having made rules in pursuance of the above-mentioned powers, which were laid before Parliament and not objected to within the forty days, the Lord Chancellor (Lord Herschell), Lord Watson, and Lord Russell of Killowen expressed the opinion, Lord Morris on this point dissenting, that it was not competent for the Courts to question the validity of the rules.

(P. 358) The LORD CHANCELLOR (Lord Herschell): . . . So far I have dealt with the question whether the rules are (p. 359) *intra vires*; but there is no doubt another very important question which has been argued before your Lordships, namely, whether this question can be canvassed in the Courts, when once the rules have been made by the Board of Trade and laid as provided on the tables of both Houses of Parliament. It is said that it is only rules properly made under sub.-s. (2) which can become part of the Act and be treated as such.

My Lords, the words of sub-s. (2) are, "The Board of

Trade shall as soon as may be after the passing of this Act, and may from time to time make such general rules as are in the opinion of the Board required for giving effect to this section, and the provisions of section 101 of the principal Act shall apply to all rules so made as if they were made in pursuance of that section." Therefore, any rule which in the opinion of the Board of Trade is required to be made in order to give effect to the section is a rule made pursuant to the provisions of sub-s. (2), and any rule made pursuant to the provisions of sub-s. (2) is to be dealt with as if made in pursuance of section 101 of the principal Act. Now, let us see what is to be the effect as regards rules made in pursuance of section 101 of the Act of 1883. First of all, "the Board of Trade may from time to time make such general rules and do such things as they think expedient", and their "general rules may be made under this section at any time after the passing of this Act, but not so as to take effect before the commencement of this Act, and shall (subject as hereinafter mentioned) be of the same effect as if they were contained in this Act, and shall be judicially noticed." The "subject as hereinafter mentioned" is this, that they are to be laid before Parliament and remain before Parliament for consideration for forty days, and during those forty days they may be annulled by a resolution of either House. If not so annulled, or until so annulled, what is the effect? They are to be "of the same effect as if they were contained in this Act". My Lords, I have asked in vain for an explanation of the meaning of those words or any suggestion as to the effect to be given to them if, notwithstanding that provision, the rules are open to review and consideration by the Courts. The effect of an enactment is that it binds all subjects who are affected by it. They are bound to conform themselves to the provisions of the law so made. The effect of a statutory rule if validly made is precisely the same, that every person must conform himself to its provisions, and if in each case a penalty be imposed, any person who does not comply with the provisions, whether of the enactment or the rule, becomes equally subject to the penalty. But there is the difference between a rule and an enactment, that whereas, apart from some such provision as we are considering, you may canvass a rule and determine whether or not it was within the power of those who made it, you cannot canvass in that way the provisions of an Act of Parliament. Therefore there is that difference between the rule and the statute. There is no difference if the rule is one within the statutory authority, but that very substantial difference if it is open to consideration whether it be so or not.

I own I feel very great difficulty in giving to this provision, that they "shall be of the same effect as if they were contained in this Act", any other meaning than this, that you shall for all purposes of construction or obligation or otherwise treat them exactly as if they were in the Act. No doubt there might be some conflict between a rule and a provision of the Act. Well, there is a conflict sometimes between two sections in the same Act. You have to try and reconcile them as best you may. If you cannot, you have to determine which is the leading provision and which the subordinate provision, and which must give way to the other. That would be so with regard to the enactment and with regard to rules which are to be treated as if within the enactment. In that case probably the enactment itself would be treated as the governing consideration and the rule as subordinate to it. Those are points that I need not dwell upon on the present occasion.

Although it is not necessary for the determination of this case to express an opinion upon it, yet, as the matter has been so much discussed, I think it only right to express the opinion which I entertain, that the words to which I have referred are really meaningless unless they have the effect which I have described, and they seem to me to be the apt and appropriate words for bringing about the effect (p. 361) which I have described. They are words, I believe, to be found in legislation only in comparatively recent years, and it is difficult to understand why they have been inserted unless with the object I have indicated.

(P. 364) LORD WATSON: . . . Now, it appears to me that the whole scheme was left to the discretion of the Board of Trade, and it is impossible for me to say that, looking at those regulations, the Board of Trade have in any measure exceeded that discretion. It was by their opinion, not by any judicial opinion, that the matter was to be determined. The Legislature retained so far a check that it required that the regulations which they framed should be laid on the table of both Houses; and of course these regulations could have been annulled by an unfavourable resolution upon a motion made in either House. But what is to be the effect if no such motion be made or carried, or if a motion hostile to the scheme be made in both Houses and rejected by both? The statute makes no difference between these cases. The views expressed by the learned judges in the Court below, so far as I understand them, would in the latter case make it competent for the Court to inquire at its own hand whether or not the Board had kept within the statute although the Legislature had declined to interfere.

But I think that all doubt upon that subject is entirely removed by the terms of section 101 of the Act of 1883, which for all practical purposes is incorporated with section 1 of the later Act. "Any rules made in pursuance (p. 365) of this section" . . . "shall be of the same effect as if they were contained in this Act, and shall be judicially noticed." My Lords, in regard to these words which I have just read, I do not think I can express my opinion more clearly than by saying that I think they mean exactly what they say. Such rules are to be as effectual as if they were part of the statute itself.

LORD MORRIS: . . . I cannot go to the further proposition which, as I understand, the noble and learned Lord on the Woolsack has laid down, that it is not competent for the Courts of Justice to consider whether these general rules are *intra vires* or *ultra vires*. I am of opinion that it is not alone competent for the Courts of Justice to consider, but that it is their duty to consider, whether the rules are *ultra vires*; that there is no power delegated by the Legislature to the Board of Trade to make any general rules which, when made, are to be considered *intra vires* provided they are laid before both Houses of Parliament, and provided that nobody has taken the trouble either to read them or to make any motion upon the subject.

. . . Now, I admit that the words are very strong; the general rules are to have the same effect as if they were embodied in the Act: I accede to that. But what general rules? General rules which are made for "giving effect" to that section; not all general rules—there is no such power in my opinion given to the Board of Trade. What are the general rules which are to have the same effect as if they were contained in the Act? The general rules made under the section—general rules such as the Legislature has, under section 101, delegated to the Board of Trade the authority of making. But if a Court of Justice (before whom all these questions must ultimately come) considers that certain rules are rules which do not come within this section, in my opinion they would be *ultra vires*, and it would be the duty of the Court not to regard them as operative. As regards the question of their receiving any further sanction from the fact of their being laid before both Houses of Parliament, that is a matter of precaution; they do not receive any imprimatur from having been laid before both Houses of Parliament; it is only that an opportunity is given to somebody or other, if he chooses to take advantage of it, of moving that they be annulled. . . .

(P. 367) LORD RUSSELL OF KILLOWEN: . . . I think that if the rules are to be read as part of the Act (as I think they ought to be) it is not, in this case, competent to judicial tribunals to reject them. Such effect must be given to them by judicial construction as can properly be given to them taking them in conjunction with the general provisions of the Act or Acts of Parliament in connection with which they have been formulated.

CHESTER *v.* BATESON, L.R. (1920), 1 K.B. 829

Reg. 2 A (2) of the Defence of the Realm Regulations was as follows: "If as respects any area in which the work of manufacturing, producing, repairing, storing, or transporting war material is being carried on, the Minister of Munitions is of opinion that the ejectment from their dwellings of workmen employed in that work is calculated to impede, delay, or restrict that work, he may by order declare the area to be a special area for the purpose of this regulation. Whilst the order remains in force no person shall, without the consent of the Minister of Munitions, take, or cause to be taken, any proceedings for the purpose of obtaining an order or decree for the recovery of possession of, or for the ejectment of a tenant of, any dwelling-house or other premises situate in the special area, being a house or premises in which any workman so employed is living, so long as the tenant continues duly to pay the rent and to observe the other conditions of the tenancy, other than any condition for the delivery up of possession. If any person acts in contravention of this regulation he shall be guilty of a summary offence against these regulations."

Held, that the making of this regulation was not a valid exercise of the power of His Majesty in Council to issue regulations for securing the public safety and the defence of the realm given by the Defence of the Realm Consolidation Act, 1914 (5 Geo. V. c. 8), section 1, and was *ultra vires*.

(P. 832) DARLING, J.: This case came before this Court

on a case stated by the justices sitting for the petty sessional division of Lonsdale North in Lancashire, and after the argument for the appellant, the respondent not being represented, we reserved judgement.

This case raises the question whether Reg. 2 A (2) goes beyond the authority by the statute 5 Geo. V. c. 8, confided to His Majesty in Council, to be exercised during the continuance of the present war for the defence of the realm. . . . The authority to make this regulation is to be found, if anywhere, in 5 Geo. V. c. 8, section 1, sub-sec. 1, par. (*e*), in the words: "Otherwise to prevent assistance being given to the enemy or the successful prosecution of the war being endangered". It is objected that the regulation is bad because it forbids any person, without the consent of the Minister of Munitions, to take or cause to be taken any proceedings to recover possession of his own house, or to eject a tenant from it, where the tenant is employed in certain work connected with war material.

Mr. Langdon has contended that this regulation violates Magna Carta, where the King declares: "To no one will we sell, to no one will we refuse or delay right or justice". I could not hold the regulation to be bad on that ground, were there sufficient authority given by a statute of the realm to those by whom the regulation was made. Magna Carta has not remained untouched; and, like every other law of England, it is not condemned to that immunity from development or improvement which was attributed to the laws of the Medes and Persians. I found my judgement rather on the passage in *R.* v. *Halliday* (1917), A.C. 268, where Lord Finlay says that Parliament may entrust great powers to His Majesty in Council, feeling certain that such powers will be reasonably exercised; and, further, on these words of Lord Atkinson in the same case: "It by no means follows, however, that if on the face of a regulation it enjoined or required something to be done which could not in any reasonable way aid in securing the public safety and the defence of the realm it would not be *ultra vires* and void. It is not necessary to decide this precise point on the present occasion, but I desire to hold myself free to deal with it when it arises." Here I think it does at last arise; and I ask myself whether it is a necessary, or even reasonable, way to aid in securing the public safety and the defence of the realm to give power to a Minister to forbid any person to institute any proceedings to recover possession of a house so long as a war worker is living in it. The main question to be decided is whether the occupant is a workman so employed, and the regulation might have been so framed as to make this a good answer to the application for possession, still leaving that question to be decided by a Court of Law. But the regulation as framed forbids the owner of the property access to all legal tribunals in regard to this matter. This might, of course, legally be done by Act of Parliament; but I think this extreme disability can be inflicted only by direct enactment of the Legislature itself, and that so grave an invasion of the rights of all subjects was not intended by the Legislature to be accomplished by a departmental order such as this one of the Minister of Munitions.

There are some instances in which Parliament has deliberately deprived certain persons of the ordinary right of citizens to resort to the King's Courts for the righting of alleged wrongs. The most notorious of these is the Vexatious Actions Act, 1896, which provides: "It shall be lawful for the Attorney-General to apply to the High Court for an order under this Act, and if he satisfies the Court that any person has habitually and persistently instituted vexatious legal proceedings without any reasonable ground for instituting such proceedings, whether in the High Court or in any inferior Court, and whether against the same person or against different persons, the Court may, after hearing such person or giving him an opportunity of being heard, after assigning counsel in case such person is unable on account of poverty to retain counsel, order that no (p. 834) legal proceedings shall be instituted by that person in the High Court or any other Court, unless he obtains the leave of the High Court or some judge thereof, and satisfies the Court or judge that such legal proceeding is not an abuse of the process of the Court, and that there is *prima facie* ground for such proceeding. A copy of such order shall be published in the *London Gazette*." Let it be observed how carefully, even when so high an official as the King's Attorney-General intervenes, resort to the Courts of Justice is preserved, and contrast this with the power of veto uncontrolled which is claimed for the Minister of Munitions.

This exceptional statute has been already enforced, as may be seen by reference to *In re Boaler* (1915), 1 K.B. 21, 36. In giving judgement in that case, Scrutton, J., used these words: "One of the valuable rights of every subject of the King is to appeal to the King in his Courts if he alleges that a civil wrong has been done to him, or if he alleges that a wrong punishable criminally has been done to him, or has been committed by another subject of the King. This right is sometimes abused, and it is, of course, quite competent to Parliament to deprive any subject of the King of it either absolutely or in part. But the language of any such statute should be jealously watched by the Courts, and should not be extended beyond its least onerous meaning unless clear words are used to justify such extension." It is to be observed that this regulation not only deprives the subject of his ordinary right to seek justice in the Courts of Law, but provides that merely to resort there without the permission of the Minister of Munitions first had and obtained shall of itself be a summary offence, and so render the seeker after justice liable to imprisonment and fine. I allow that in stress of war we may rightly be obliged, as we should be ready, to forgo much of our liberty, but I hold that this elemental right of the subjects of the British Crown cannot be thus easily taken from them. Should we hold that the permit of a departmental official is a necessary condition precedent for a subject of the realm who would demand justice at the (p. 835) seat of judgement, the people would be in that unhappy condition indicated, but not anticipated, by Montesquieu, in *De l'Esprit des Lois*, where he writes: "Les Anglais pour favoriser la liberté ont ôté toutes les puissances intermédiaires qui formoient leur monarchie. Ils ont bien raison de conserver cette liberté; s'ils venoient à la perdre, ils seroient un des peuples les plus esclaves de la terre" (Livre 2, c. 4).

Avory, J.: . . . The effect of this regulation is that, if any person without the previous consent of the Minister of Munitions commences proceedings in any of the King's Courts of Justice of the kind prohibited, he is guilty of a criminal offence and liable to six months' imprisonment or a fine of £100, or both; and the only question for decision is whether this portion of the regulation is *ultra vires* the statute under which it purports to be made, that is to say, the Defence of the Realm Consolidation Act, 1914. This depends upon whether it can be said, on any reasonable construction of the statute, to be a regulation for securing the public safety and the defence of the realm, and, particularly under section 1, sub-sec. (1) (*e*), whether it can be said to be a regulation to prevent the successful prosecution of the war being endangered; the latter being probably the most plausible ground on which it might be supported. We have not had the advantage of hearing any argument in support of it, nor are we favoured with the grounds of the decision of the justices. The purpose in view when the regulation was made, namely, to prevent the disturbance of munition workers in their dwellings, may, without doubt (p. 836), be said to be reasonable; and a regulation, designed to prevent such disturbance, providing that no order for ejectment should be made except under conditions prescribed, would probably be held to be *intra vires* the statute; but the objection which is made to the regulation as it stands is that it deprives the King's subjects of their right of access to the Courts of Justice, and renders them liable to punishment if they have the temerity to ask for justice in any of the King's Courts. It is not difficult to conceive a case in which a landlord might honestly believe that the rent had not been paid, or some other condition of the tenancy had been violated by the tenant, which would justify him in applying to a Court of Justice for an order of ejectment without the consent of the Minister of Munitions; but if it should be determined that he was mistaken, either in law or fact, he would be liable to punishment for having instituted the proceedings. In my opinion there is not to be found in the statute anything to authorize or justify a regulation having that result; and nothing less than express words in the statute taking away the right of the King's subjects of access to the Courts of Justice would authorize or justify it.

I have based my judgement solely upon the construction of the statute which confers the power to make regulations. If the question had to be determined as a question of constitutional law, I should agree that this regulation is in conflict with, and in violation of, the provisions of Magna Carta, cc. 39 and 40; of the Bill of Rights (1 W. & M. Sess. 2, c. 2, s. 1), which provides that the pretended power of suspending the laws or the execution of laws by regal authority without the consent of Parliament is illegal; and particularly, it would be a violation of the statute of Northampton, 2 Edw. III. c. 8, which provides: "It is accorded and established that it shall not be commanded by the great seal nor the little seal to disturb or delay common right; and though such commandings do come, the justices shall not therefore leave to do right in any point"—"shall not leave to do right" means shall not omit to do right—"notwithstanding that there is a commanding under the great or little seal." In this connection I think it is not inappropriate to quote a passage from the opinion, though (p. 337) it is a dissentient opinion, of Lord Shaw of Dunfermline, in the case of *R.* v. *Halliday*, where he says: "Whether the Government has exceeded its statutory mandate is a question of *ultra* or *intra vires* such as that which is now being tried. In so far as the mandate has been exceeded, there lurk the elements of a transition to arbitrary government, and therein of grave constitutional and public danger. The increasing crush of legislative efforts, and the convenience to the Executive of a refuge to the device of Orders in Council, would increase that danger tenfold were the judiciary to approach any such action of the Government in a spirit of compliance rather than of independent scrutiny." For these reasons I hold this part of the regulation to be *ultra vires* and invalid. . . .

SANKEY, J.: . . . In my view the words in the statute relied upon as giving power to His Majesty to make this regulation do not enable him to do so, nor is there anything in the Act of 1914 which authorized the making of regulations forbidding access to the King's Courts. It is (p. 838) true that the power to make a regulation to prevent the successful prosecution of the war being endangered is of a wide and sweeping character, but I decline to hold that Parliament intended to give to the Executive the right to close any of the King's Courts against his subjects unless they obtained the sanction of a Minister to resort thereto.

It might have been competent under the words of the

statute, although I express no opinion on the point, to make regulations constituting the consent of the Minister of Munitions, in a proper case, a condition precedent to the making of an order for the recovery of the possession of, or for the ejectment of a tenant of, any dwelling-house or other premises of the character referred to. It was not, however, competent for His Majesty in Council to make a regulation enacting that a man who seeks the assistance of, or the protection of, the King's Courts should be exposed to fine and imprisonment for having done so. It would have been astonishing if Parliament had conferred such a power as that. See what would have happened in a doubtful case. A man believing in all good faith that he was entitled to bring proceedings finds he is wrong on the evidence, but the mere fact of his having brought them is to make him guilty of an offence and liable to fine and imprisonment. I am of opinion that the regulation so made is beyond the powers conferred by the Act of Parliament. I should be slow to hold that Parliament ever conferred such a power unless it expressed it in the clearest possible language, and should never hold that it was given indirectly by ambiguous regulations made in pursuance of any Act.

R. *v.* HOME SECRETARY, *ex parte* O'BRIEN, L.R. (1923), 2 K.B. 361

The Restoration of Order in Ireland Act, 1920 (10 & 11 Geo. V. c. 31), sec. 1, sub-sec. (1), empowered His Majesty in Council to issue regulations for securing the restoration and maintenance of order in Ireland. By Reg. 14 B made under this Act: "Where on the recommendation of a competent naval or military authority or of one of the advisory committees hereinafter mentioned it appears to the Secretary of State that for securing the restoration or maintenance of order in Ireland it is expedient that a person who is suspected of acting or having acted or being about to act in a manner prejudicial to the restoration or maintenance of order in Ireland shall be subjected to such obligations and restrictions as are hereinafter mentioned, the Secretary of State may by order require that person forthwith, or from time to time, either to remain in, or to proceed to and reside in, such place as may be specified in the order. . . . Any person interned under such order shall be subject to the like restrictions and may be dealt with in like manner as a prisoner of war. . . . An order under this regulation may require the person to whom the order relates to reside or to be interned in any place in the British Islands."

On December 5, 1922, the Irish Free State Constitution Act (13 Geo. V. Sess. 2, c. 1) was passed, giving the Irish Free State a separate Executive.

On March 7, 1923, the Home Secretary made an order under the said Reg. 14B, that Mr. Art O'Brien, who was then resident in England, should be interned in the Irish Free State in such place as the Irish Free State Government might determine, and should be subject to all rules and conditions applicable to persons there interned and should remain there until further order. Under this order Mr. O'Brien was arrested in London and taken to Mountjoy Prison in Dublin, and there detained in custody. The

Free State Government had agreed with the Home Secretary that if an advisory committee appointed for the purpose of the regulation should decide that he ought not to have been deported, he would be released.

In an application on behalf of Mr. O'Brien for a writ of habeas corpus directed to the Home Secretary, it was held by the Court of Appeal that Reg. 14B was impliedly repealed by the Irish Free State Constitution Act, and the order for internment was therefore illegal, and that in view of the agreement between the Home Secretary and the Irish Free State Government, the writ ought to issue addressed to the Home Secretary.

(P. 375) BANKES L.J.: . . . The questions for decision in the present case may be divided under three heads: (1) Whether since the establishment of the Irish Free State an order can be lawfully made by the Home Secretary for the internment in that State of a person at the date of the order residing in England? (2) Whether, assuming that such an order can lawfully be made, the order now complained of is in form a compliance with the regulation? (3) Whether the application for a writ of habeas corpus directed to the Home Secretary is the proper procedure under the circumstances of the case? It is inconceivable that the order for the internment of the applicant could have been made by the Home Secretary unless he had before him information which in his opinion not only justified, but required, the making of the order; presumably also in a matter of this importance he acted upon advice as to his powers. It is a matter of regret therefore that the Court should have been called upon to consider the legality of his action. The Court knows nothing of the facts upon which the Home Secretary acted, and even if it did it could have no right to be influenced by them. The duty of the Court is clear. The liberty of a subject is in question. The Court must inquire, and inquire closely, into the question whether the order of (p. 376) internment complained of was or was not lawfully made. . . . It is quite clear . . . that the Executive of the Irish Free State is an Executive distinct from and independent of the Executive in England, just as distinct and just as independent as the Executive of the Dominion of Canada is from the Executive of England. . . . The regulation confers upon a branch of the Executive in England certain absolute powers, and among them the absolute power of interning persons without trial, and without (p. 377) informing them of the details of the charge made against them, or of the evidence upon which it is made, and for an unlimited period. The regulation is silent in reference to any power of discharge or release, but it is obvious that such a power must be implied. In whom is the implied power vested? Obviously, as it seems to me, in the branch of the Executive by whom the power to intern was exercised. . . . I confess to a difficulty in attaching any definite meaning to so much of this regulation as refers to the manner in which a prisoner of war may be dealt with. It must, I think, refer to the manner in which a prisoner of war is dealt with in the country the Executive of which makes the order of internment. . . . There can be no possible doubt as to the modification of restrictions, as the regulation provides that they can only be modified by the Secretary of State. These provisions to my mind point irresistibly to the conclusion that since the establishment of the Irish Free State an order cannot lawfully be made by the Home Secretary for the internment of a person in the Irish Free State. The reasons appear to me to be these (p. 378). In the first place, because the order deprives the Executive of this country of that full and uncontrolled right to direct the release of the interned person which in my opinion is a necessary incident of a valid order of internment under the regulation; secondly, because the effect of the order is to subject the interned person to restrictions other than those indicated in the regulation and to restrictions which the Secretary of State has no power to modify; and, thirdly, because the interned person is deprived of the particular form of trial which is prescribed by the regulations in the event of his committing any of the offences indicated in the regulation. The view which I have just expressed as to the construction and effect of the regulation is strongly borne out by that part of the regulation which expressly provides that an order under the regulation may require the person to whom the order relates to reside or to be interned in any place in the British Islands. The fact that in August 1920, when this regulation was made, it was thought necessary to make such a provision is, I consider, a powerful argument in support of the contention of the applicant in the present case. . . .

(P. 381) The last point for consideration is whether a writ ought to be issued directed to the Home Secretary having regard to the contention of the Attorney-General, which was accepted by the Divisional Court, that as the applicant was deported to and was interned in the Irish Free State the Home Secretary had no longer any power or control over him except in so far as the Government of that State had agreed that, in the event of the advisory committee deciding that he ought not to have been deported and interned, they could release him. . . . This question cannot, I think, be satisfactorily disposed of unless the rule is made absolute, which will give the Home Secretary the opportunity, if he desires to take advantage of it, of making the position clearer than at present it appears to be. . . . The order, therefore, is made absolute.

(P. 382) In conclusion it may not be out of place to observe upon the practice of legislation by means of Orders in Council that, though the practice may be a convenience to Parliament, it is one which leads to inconvenience and difficulties and dangers of which the present case is only one example. Laws are made the drafting of which has never been subjected to criticism in Parliament, and when made they are not included in the Statute Book. The result is that in the first place they are difficult to find, and when found they are more often than not difficult of interpretation, whether it be by a lawyer who is called upon to interpret them, or by a Minister of the Crown whose duty it is to administer them.

SCRUTTON, L.J.: This appeal raises questions of great importance regarding the liberty of the subject, a matter on which English law is anxiously careful, and which English judges are keen to uphold. As Lord Herschell says in *Cox* v. *Hakes* (15 App. Cas. 506, 527): "The law of this country has been very jealous of any infringement of personal liberty". This care is not to be exercised less vigilantly because the subject whose liberty is in question may not be particularly meritorious. It is indeed one test of belief in principles if you apply them to cases with which you have no sympathy at all. You really believe in freedom of speech if you are willing to allow it to men whose opinions seem to you wrong and even dangerous; and the subject is entitled only to be deprived of his liberty by due process of law, although that due process if taken will probably send him to prison. A man undoubtedly guilty of murder must yet be released if due forms of law have not been followed in his conviction. It is quite possible, even probable, that the subject in this case is guilty of high treason; he is still entitled only to be deprived of his liberty by due process of law. . . .

(P. 387) If . . . before the Irish Free State Constitution Act a Secretary of State could order internment in Ireland, the continuance of this power is inconsistent with the creation of an Irish Executive in the same position as that of the Dominion of Canada, and having in consequence exclusive executive jurisdiction within its territory. Therefore no such order could be made by a Secretary of State after the passing of the Irish Free State Constitution Act, because the previous law allowing it was inconsistent with the provisions of the Irish Constitution so far as they created an Irish Executive, and that previous law was therefore repealed. The power also ceased to exist because the regulations did not allow internment by order in a place where the person ordering had no control of the internment, and the creation of the Constitution had converted

Ireland into such a place as regards the power of control of the Secretary of State. . . .

(P. 391) There remains the question whether a writ of habeas corpus is the appropriate remedy for the illegality of the order and detention. . . .

Now it has been laid down by the House of Lords in *Barnardo* v. *Ford* (1892), A.C. 326, that if the Court is satisfied that the body whose production is asked is not in the custody, power, or control of the person to whom it is sought to address the writ, a writ of habeas corpus is not the proper remedy, though there was an original illegal taking and detention. The object of the writ is not to (p. 393) punish previous illegality, but to release from present illegal detention. . . . It may be that on hearing that in the opinion of this Court the order was issued without legal authority, the Home Secretary, with the assistance of the Irish Free State Government, will produce the body, as it is hardly in the interests of either Government to act illegally. . . .

(P. 393) Atkin, L. J.: . . . The case involves questions of grave constitutional importance, upon which I feel bound to express my own opinion, even though I repeat to some extent the views already expressed by the other members of the Court. That a British subject resident in England should be exposed to summary arrest, transport to Ireland, and imprisonment there without any conviction or order of a Court of Justice, is an occurrence which has to be justified by the Minister responsible. . . .

(P. 394) Apart from the effect of the creation of the Irish Free State it cannot, I think, be disputed that the powers of making regulations given by the Restoration of Order in Ireland Act, 1920, included the power to make Reg. 14B (*R.* v. *Halliday* (1917), A.C. 260), nor can it be disputed in this Court that the regulation empowers the Home Secretary to exercise in England the powers given under it (*Ex parte* Brady, 91 L.J. (K.B.), 98), a decision (p. 395) which binds me and therefore which I do not discuss. . . . When I consider the effect upon this regulation of the Irish Free State Constitution Act, 1922, I am forced to the conclusion that the executive powers given to the Ministers named in the regulation and essential for the efficiency of any order for internment in Ireland no longer exist. . . .

(P. 396) I think, therefore, that Reg. 14B, so far as it relates to a power to intern in the Irish Free State, is repealed by the Irish Free State Constitution Act. . . .

Having come to this conclusion on the broad constitutional point, I need not deal at much length with the other points raised. But even if there were otherwise power to order a person to be interned in Ireland, I am of opinion that the absence of any power to modify the restrictions incident to internment would in itself be fatal to the validity of the order.

(P. 397) Moreover, I think that the Home Secretary had no power to order the applicant to be interned "in such place as the Irish Free State Government may determine". This seems to me to be the very contrary of a place "specified". The choice of place obviously determines the conditions and restrictions under which the subject is confined, and in my opinion the Home Secretary had no more right to delegate the choice of place to the Irish Free State Government than to the first man he met in the street. I think that on this ground also the order is invalid.

(P. 398) Having come to the definite conclusion that the order made by the Home Secretary is invalid and that the imprisonment of the applicant thereunder is unlawful, it only remains to consider whether the writ should go to the Home Secretary. I think that the question is whether there is evidence that the Home Secretary has the custody or control of the applicant. Actual physical custody is (p. 399) obviously not essential. . . . It seems to me that much support for the contention that the Home Secretary retains *de facto* control is afforded by the words of the order itself, a copy of which is served on the applicant. The order is that the applicant shall "be interned in the Irish Free State . . . and shall remain there until further orders". It was conceded that the ordinary interpretation of those words would be until further orders by the Home Secretary, though it was said that in fact he had no power to give such orders. I cannot without further explanation accept this. The order proceeds: "If I am satisfied by the report of the Committee that this order may be revoked or varied without injury to the restoration and maintenance of order in Ireland I will revoke or vary this order by a further order in writing under my hand. Failing such revocation or variation this order shall remain in force." I cannot explain these provisions on the footing that there is no *de facto* control. In this case it is plain that the applicant was at one time in the custody and control of the Home Secretary by an order which we have held to be illegal. There is, to say the least, grave doubt whether he is not still in the custody or control of the Home Secretary. The case of *Barnardo* v. *Ford* appears to me to afford ample ground for the conclusion that this Court should order the writ to go addressed to the Home Secretary in order that he may deal fully with the matter, and if he has in fact parted with control, show fully how that has come about. The rule must be made absolute.

R. *v.* Electricity Commissioners, L.R. (1924), 1 K.B. 171

The Electricity (Supply) Act, 1919, 9 & 10 Geo. V. c. 100), sections 5, 6, empowered the Electricity Commissioners to formulate schemes for the improvement of the existing organization for the supply of electricity in electricity districts, and, where necessary, for the formation of a joint electricity authority for a district, and directed them to hold local inquiries on the schemes. By section 7 (1) the Commissioners were empowered to make an order giving effect to the schemes embodying decisions arrived at as the result of the local inquiry, and present the order for confirmation by the Board of Trade (now the Minister of Transport), who might confirm the order with or without modification as they thought fit; and by section 7 (2) "Any such order shall be laid, as soon as may be after it is confirmed, before each House of Parliament, but shall not come into operation unless and until it has been approved either with or without modification by a resolution passed by each such House, and when so approved shall have effect as if enacted in this Act. . . ."

The Commissioners formulated a scheme in purported exercise of their powers, and were proceeding to hold a local inquiry with a view to making an order giving effect to the scheme. On an application for writs of prohibition and certiorari, it was held by the Court of Appeal that, the scheme being *ultra vires*, a writ of prohibition should issue, prohibiting the Commissioners from proceeding with the further consideration of the scheme.

(P. 189) BANKES, L.J.: . . . The important part of the appeal has reference to the jurisdiction of the Court to make any order either for prohibition or certiorari. The first objection taken was that any application was premature (p. 190), the matter being still only in its opening stage. The Commissioners, it was said, have decided nothing; they have merely published the scheme preparatory to holding the local inquiry thereon which they are directed by section 5, sub-section (4), of the Act of 1919 to hold before making any order. This objection may be a valid objection to the granting of a writ of certiorari, but as it is not necessary to decide the point I express no opinion upon it. With regard to prohibition, if the writ lies at all I do not think that the objection is a sound one. . . .

The other objections to granting any writ were much more serious, and they raise difficult and important questions, constitutional as well as legal. In substance, the objections come to this: (*a*) that the proceedings of the Electricity Commissioners are of an executive and not a judicial character; (*b*) that whether that be so or not, their (p. 191) proceedings in reference to the preparation of schemes, as directed by the Electricity Act, 1919, are controllable by Parliament, and by Parliament alone, and are such that there is no moment of time at which the Court can intervene to inquire whether the proceedings are *ultra vires* or not. The argument on this second contention is presented in the following way: Section 7 of the Act, it is said, provides that the Commissioners may make an order giving effect to a scheme, but that order has no force or effect in itself. It is merely a suggestion or advice to be passed on to the Minister of Transport, who may confirm or modify the scheme. Even then the order has no force. It must first be approved by resolution passed by each House of Parliament, and then, and not till then, has the order any force or effect. As soon as the order has been approved by both Houses of Parliament the section provides that it shall have effect as if enacted in the Act. The result, according to the respondents, is that any application to the Court for a writ of prohibition or certiorari must be either premature or too late: premature if made before the order of the Commissioners becomes an Act of Parliament, too late if made after it has attained that status. This argument has only become possible since the Legislature has adopted the practice of providing that resolutions or orders which are directed to lie on the table for a certain period before becoming effective, or which have to be approved by resolution of the Houses of Parliament, are, when approved, to have effect as if they were themselves Acts of Parliament. The effect of legislation in this form was discussed in the case of *Institute of Patent Agents* v. *Lockwood* (1894), A.C. 347, 365, where Lord Watson concludes his speech by saying: "Such rules are to be as effectual as if they were part of the statute itself". The effect of accepting the argument of the Attorney-General on this point would be very far-reaching. It would amount to a decision that the subject has no longer the right in cases like the present, where this form of legislation is adopted, to come to a Court of Law and demand an inquiry whether the action, or decision, of which he is (p. 192) complaining is *ultra vires* or not. I question very much whether Parliament had any deliberate intention of producing the result by adopting this particular form of legislation.

I pass now to consider the contention that if the Court makes an order in the present case for the issue of a writ of prohibition it will be trespassing on ground reserved by Parliament to itself. I cannot see why this action of the Court should be so regarded. By the Act of 1919 Parliament laid down the limits of the jurisdiction of the Electricity Commissioners. It did so presumably because it considered that those limits were the proper ones, and the ones which the Commissioners should observe. Why should Parliament object to a Court of Law, if appealed to, using its powers to keep the Commissioners within those limits? Parliament no doubt has, as between itself and the Commissioners, provided that no order of the Commissioners shall have effect unless first approved by Parliament. This reservation must, I consider, be treated as a reservation for the purposes of control, and does not in my opinion exclude the jurisdiction of the Courts of Law. If any decision of a Court of Law in the opinion of Parliament unduly fetters the action of the Commissioners, it is always open to Parliament to extend the limits of that jurisdiction.

I have so far only dealt in a general way with the arguments addressed to the Court by the Attorney-General. The real question is whether the principles already down in reference to the power and duty of the Courts to issue writs of prohibition apply to the present case. There can, of course, be no exact precedent, as the Electricity Commissioners are a body of quite recent creation. It has, however, always been the boast of our common law that it will, whenever possible, and where necessary, apply existing principles to new sets of circumstances. . . .

(P. 198) The conclusion I have come to in reference to the whole matter is that there is abundant precedent for the Court taking action at the present stage of the proceedings of the Electricity Commissioners, provided it is satisfied that the Commissioners are proceeding judicially in making their report, even though that report needs the confirmation of the Minister of Transport and of both Houses of Parliament before it becomes effective. In coming to a conclusion on this latter point it is necessary to deal with the case on its own particular circumstances. The Electricity Act of 1919 imposes upon the Electricity Commissioners very wide and very responsible duties and power in reference to the approval or formulation of schemes. At every stage they are required to hold local inquiries for the purpose of giving interested parties the opportunity of being heard. Their authority extends to the creation of bodies who may exercise all or any of the powers of the authorized undertakers within the electricity district, and to whom the undertakings themselves may be transferred on terms settled by the Commissioners. On principle and on authority it is in my opinion open to this Court to hold, and I consider that it should hold, that powers so far-reaching, affecting as they do individuals as well as property, are powers to be exercised judicially, and not ministerially or merely, to use the language of Palles, C.B., as proceedings towards legislation. On these grounds I consider that the appeal against the order of the Divisional Court discharging the rule *nisi* for a prohibition must be allowed with costs here and below, and the rule for prohibition in the terms of the rule *nisi* must be made absolute. The appeal against the order refusing to make the rule *nisi* for a certiorari absolute is dismissed without costs.

(P. 204) ATKIN, L.J.: . . . The question now arises whether the persons interested are entitled to the remedy which they now claim in order to put a stop to the unauthorized proceedings of the Commissioners. The matter comes before us upon rules for writs of prohibition and certiorari which have been discharged by the Divisional Court. Both writs are of great antiquity, forming part of the process by which the King's Courts restrained Courts of inferior jurisdiction from exceeding their powers. Prohibition restrains the tribunal from proceeding further in excess of jurisdiction; certiorari requires the record or the order of the Court to be sent up to the King's Bench Division, to have its legality inquired into, and, if necessary, to have the order quashed. It is to be noted that both writs deal with questions of excessive jurisdiction, and doubtless in their origin dealt almost exclusively with the jurisdiction of what is described in ordinary parlance as a Court of Justice. But the operation of the writs has extended to control the proceedings of bodies which do not claim to be, and would not be recognized as, Courts of Justice. Wherever any body of persons having legal authority to determine questions affecting the rights of subjects, and having the duty to act judicially, act in excess of their legal authority they are subject to the controlling jurisdiction of the King's Bench Division (p. 206) exercised in these writs. . . . I can see no difference in principle between certiorari and prohibition, except that the latter may be invoked at an earlier stage. If the proceedings establish that the body complained of is exceeding its jurisdiction by entertaining matters which would result in its final decision being subject to being brought up and quashed on certiorari, I think that prohibition will lie to restrain it from so exceeding its jurisdiction. . . .

(P. 207) It is necessary, however, to deal with what I think was the main objection of the Attorney-General. In this case he said the Commissioners come to no decision at all. They recommend an order embodying a scheme to the Minister of Transport, who may confirm it with or without modifications. Similarly the Minister of Transport comes to no decision. He submits the order to the Houses of Parliament, who may approve it with or without modifications. The Houses of Parliament may put anything into the order they please, whether consistent with the Act of 1919 or not. Until they have approved, nothing is decided, and in truth the whole procedure, draft scheme, inquiry, order, confirmation, approval, is only part of a process by which Parliament is expressing its will, and at no stage is subject to any control by the Courts. It is unnecessary to emphasize the constitutional importance of this contention. Given its full effect, it means that the checks and safeguards which have been imposed by Act of Parliament, including the freedom from compulsory (p. 208) taking, can be removed, and new and onerous and inconsistent obligations imposed without an Act of Parliament, and by simple resolution of both Houses of Parliament. I do not find it necessary to determine whether, on the proper construction of the statute, resolutions of the two Houses of Parliament could have the effect claimed. In the provision that the final decision of the Commissioners is not to be operative until it has been approved by the two Houses of Parliament I find nothing inconsistent with the view that in arriving at that decision the Commissioners themselves are to act judicially and within the limits prescribed by Act of Parliament, and that the Courts have power to keep them within those limits. It is to be noted that it is the order of the Commissioners that eventually takes effect; neither the Minister of Transport who confirms, nor the Houses of Parliament who approve, can under the statute make an order which in respect of the matters in question has any operation. . . .

(P. 212) YOUNGER, L.J.: . . . That Act (the Act of 1919) in my judgement contemplates that the Commissioners' order, which, when approved by a resolution passed by each House of Parliament, is to have effect as if enacted in the Act, embodies only a scheme which under the Act the Commissioners are given power either to approve or formulate. Every scheme under the Act remains the scheme of the Commissioners even after it is confirmed by the Minister of Transport and approved by Parliament. The modifications in a scheme inserted either by the Minister of Transport or by Parliament are limited to modifications, as I read the Act, which might have been lawfully made under the powers of the Act by the Commissioners themselves had they been so minded. Parliament has not by the Act conferred upon the Minister of Transport, nor has it in terms reserved to itself by a mere resolution of both Houses power, under the name of modifications in a scheme of the Commissioners, to insert in a scheme provisions which would under the Act be beyond the powers of the Commissioners if inserted by them in the scheme in the first instance. So, at any rate, I read the Act. Fortunately, however, it is not necessary in this case to decide the very serious question whether, if at any time Parliament should approve by resolution of each House a scheme (p. 213) which, adopting if I may the language of Lord Robertson in *Russell* v. *Magistrates of Hamilton*, 25 R. 350, 357, could in fact be shown to be "an abuse" of the statute, the scheme so approved would nevertheless by virtue of section 7, sub-section (2), "have effect as if enacted in this Act", and would have to be given statutory force by every Court in which its terms were canvassed. To suggest that such a question is one which may in view of the terms of this sub-section arise, is not of course to suggest that Parliament cannot sanction and give the effect of statute law to any scheme it likes. It is only to suggest that it may not have in this Act reserved to itself the power by a mere resolution of each House to give statutory effect to a scheme the formulation of which it has not by the statute authorized. No such serious question, however, arises for decision now. For the moment it is, I think, enough to say that, whatever may be the effect of a joint resolution when once it is passed, Parliament in this statute contemplates that no such resolution will approve, except possibly by inadvertence, a scheme which it would under the Act be beyond the powers of the Commissioners to formulate or of the Minister of Transport to confirm. If that be the true view of the statute, the interference of the Court in such a case as this, and at this stage, so far from being even in the most diluted sense of the words a challenge to its supremacy, will be of an assistance to Parliament. It will relieve each House to some extent at least from the risk of having presented to it for approval by resolution schemes which go beyond the powers committed by the statute to the Commissioners who made them or the Minister of Transport who confirmed them. It will leave each House to a great extent untrammelled by any apprehensions of this kind, to devote itself to the consideration of the question the Act has undoubtedly reserved to it—namely, whether in the particular case the scheme should be approved or not. For these reasons I am of opinion that if we have the power in this case to interfere, we are rendering a service not only to the parties concerned but to each House of Parliament itself by exercising that power as we propose to do.

BOARD OF EDUCATION *v.* RICE,
L.R. (1911), Appeal Cases, 179

Section 7, sub-s. (3), of the Education Act, 1902 (2 Ed. VII. c. 42), provides that "If any question arises under this section between the local education authority and the managers of a school not provided by the authority, that question shall be determined by the Board of Education". The Board was required under this sub-section to determine: "(1) Whether the local education authority have in fixing and paying the salaries of the teachers fulfilled their duty under sub-s. (1) of sec. 7 of the Act. (2) Whether the salaries inserted in the teachers' present agreements are reasonable in amount and ought to be paid by the authority, or what salaries the authority ought to pay." The Board having purported to decide these questions by a document which did not dispose of them, it was held that the purported decision must be brought up by writ of certiorari and quashed, and that a writ of mandamus must issue commanding the Board to determine the questions.

(P. 180) The LORD CHANCELLOR (Lord Loreburn): . . . It is unnecessary to enter into detail upon the protracted dispute between the Swansea Local Education Authority and the managers of the Oxford Street voluntary schools, technically termed "non-provided" schools. Certain salaries were paid to teachers by the local education authority in the "provided" schools within their area. Smaller salaries had been paid to the teachers in the voluntary schools prior to the Act of 1902, and, after that Act passed, the same system of paying smaller salaries was continued.

Then some of the teachers gave notice upon the ground that their salaries were inadequate and below those paid to their comrades in the provided schools. And the managers of the Oxford Street schools pressed upon the local education authority the fact that they were able to keep their teachers only by finding out of their own pockets, or by the assistance of well-wishers, the difference between the two scales of salary. They claimed that by refusing to level up those salaries to the same scale the local education authority had failed to discharge its statutory duty of maintaining and keeping efficient the Oxford Street schools. Mr. Hamilton, K.C., who was sent down to inquire and report to the Board of Education in London (p. 181), reported that there had been such a failure. And upon all the evidence before the House there can be no manner of doubt that he was right. . . .

I proceed now to consider what is the statutory duty laid upon the Board of Education in regard to disputes of this kind.

Their duties, so far as concerns the present litigation, are twofold. In the first place they are required by s. 7, sub-s. (3), of the Act of 1902 to determine a certain class of questions. The words of the sub-section run as follows: "If any question arises under this section between the local education authority and the managers of a school not provided by the authority, that question shall be determined by the Board of Education".

The Attorney-General argued, as I understood him, that the questions then pointed at are only such as arise from the statutory relations between a local education authority and managers, and are not such as arise from the duty of one or other towards the public. He contended that the duty of maintaining and keeping efficient a non-provided school, though it is in terms imposed by s. 7 of the Act, is not a matter which can be a "question" between the local education authority and the managers, so as to come within the jurisdiction of the Board. I cannot accept this view. The managers are directly interested in the proper maintenance. And I do not understand how it can be held that if they do so call upon the local education authority, and the latter disputes the point, it is not a question arising between them. Equally I fail to understand how it can be held that such a question is not one arising under s. 7 (p. 182), for it is only under s. 7 that the duty is created. And all questions arising under s. 7 are to be determined by the Board of Education by virtue of the third sub-section.

Comparatively recent statutes have extended, if they have not originated, the practice of imposing upon departments or officers of State the duty of deciding or determining questions of various kinds. In the present instance, as in many others, what comes for determination is sometimes a matter to be settled by discretion, involving no law. It will, I suppose, usually be of an administrative kind; but sometimes it will involve matter of law as well as matter of fact, or even depend upon matter of law alone. In such cases the Board of Education will have to ascertain the law and also to ascertain the facts. I need not add that in doing either they must act in good faith and fairly listen to both sides, for that is a duty lying upon everyone who decides anything. But I do not think they are bound to treat such a question as though it were a trial. They have no power to administer an oath, and need not examine witnesses. They can obtain information in any way they think best, always giving a fair opportunity to those who are parties in the controversy for correcting or contradicting any relevant statement prejudicial to their view. Provided this is done, there is no appeal from the determination of the Board under s. 7, sub-s. (3), of this Act. The Board have, of course, no jurisdiction to decide abstract questions of law, but only to determine actual concrete differences that may arise, and as they arise, between the managers and the local education authority. The Board is in the nature of the arbitral tribunal, and a Court of Law has no jurisdiction to hear appeals from the determination either upon law or upon fact. But if the Court is satisfied either that the Board have not acted judicially in the way I have described, or have not determined the question which they are required by the Act to determine, then there is a remedy by mandamus and certiorari.

In the second place the Board are authorized, by s. 16 of the Act of 1902, to make such order as they think necessary or proper for the purpose of compelling the local (p. 183) education authority to fulfil its duty, if after holding a public inquiry they think it has failed to fulfil any of its duties under the Act of 1902. This is a perfectly distinct thing from what is prescribed by s. 7, sub-s. (3). It is designed to enable the Board of Education, if they think it right, to make an order and to enforce by application to the Courts of Law obedience to such order as they may make. It does not deal with the determination of disputes between a local education authority and managers, though if such dispute is decided one way and the local education authority refused to act in accordance with the decision, its refusal may be followed by an order under s. 16 and by an application to the Court to enforce it. In the coil in which this quarrel, simple as it is in itself, has been entangled, this distinction may have been somewhat overlooked. . . .

(P. 184) Such being the duties of the Board of Education, I next inquire what it is that they have done. They have purported to determine a question under s. 7, sub-s. (3), of the Act which I do not think was really that which arose between the parties. . . .

(P. 185) . . . I think there has been a confusion between the points that were to be decided and the arguments of either side, and perhaps also a confusion between the Board's duty under s. 7, sub-s. (3), and their duty under s. 16. The managers were entitled to an explicit determination of the questions which they raised. This they have not obtained. . . . That suffices to dispose of the case, and I move your Lordships to dismiss this appeal with costs.

EARL OF HALSBURY: My Lords, I am of opinion that this judgement ought to be affirmed. The duty of the education authority was to keep the schools efficient; this duty they neglected, and did not keep the schools efficient. The local (p. 186) education authority assumed to itself an absolute autocratic authority as to what schools they would keep efficient, and I cannot doubt for myself that they thought they were entitled to starve the Church schools and give advantages to the provided schools which they would not grant to the Church schools. . . .

(P. 187) LORD ATKINSON: My Lords, I concur in both the judgements which have been delivered.

LORD SHAW OF DUNFERMLINE: My Lords, I concur in the judgement of the Lord Chancellor, and I desire to add two statements in the light of which this concurrence will, I trust, be read.

With regard to the local education authority, that authority is not before us, and we have not had the advantage of hearing their views presented at your Lordships' Bar. Speaking, therefore, for myself, I am not satisfied that any observation reflecting upon their conduct would be justified from me.

On the point of discrimination, my Lords, I desire to say this, that where the circumstances are the same, discrimination primarily requires justification. But, on the other hand, this state of circumstances, that is to say, a state of complete similarity—in the varying conditions as to schools, staffs, localities, and otherwise—may be most infrequent, and to apply the same standard to dissimilar circumstances is, in my humble judgement, itself such a discrimination as would also require justification.

The point really underlying these two questions which are now remitted to be answered is whether in the individual case, and apart altogether from reference to other cases, or to a general standard, efficient education has or has not been provided in the particular school. To that as the ultimate issue the attention of the parties must be directed. I do not doubt that the local education authority must act impartially, but upon the whole I desire to interpose these observations to my assent to the judgement proposed from the woolsack.

LORD MERSEY: My Lords, I entirely concur.

CHAPTER X

EXAMPLES FROM STATUTES

In the following pages will be found a number of sections from statutes either conferring legislative powers on, or providing for the exercise of judicial functions by, Ministers or Government departments. The sections have been selected as illustrations of some of the different forms in which such statutory provisions are framed.

The Patents, Designs, and Trade Marks Act, 1883, gave wide powers to the Board of Trade to make rules for regulating the practice of registration under the Act, and generally for regulating the business of the Patent Office. It was provided that such rules should be of the same effect as if they were contained in the Act, and should be judicially noticed, but that they should be laid before both Houses of Parliament, and if either House, within forty days after they had been so laid, resolved that such rules or any of them ought to be annulled, the same should after the date of the resolution be of no effect, without prejudice to the validity of anything done in the meantime under the rules or to the making of any new rules. It was these provisions which were in question in the case of the *Institute of Patent Agents* v. *Lockwood*.

By the Local Government Act, 1888, the Local Government Board were empowered to make such orders as appeared to them necessary for bringing the Act into operation, and by any such order to modify the provisions of that or any other Act of Parliament, so far as might appear to the Board necessary for that purpose.

Section 7 of the Education Act, 1902, provided that if any question arose under the section between a local education authority and the managers of a school not provided by the authority, the question should be determined by the Board of Education. The duties of the Board of Education in reference to the determination of questions under this provision were the subject of the decision in the case of the *Board of Education* v. *Rice*.

The Trade Marks Act, 1905, gave power to the Board of Trade to make rules and prescribe forms for regulating the practice under the Act with respect to trade marks, and the Patents and Designs Act, 1907, gave similar powers to the Board of Trade with respect to designs. Both of these Acts contained the same kind of provisions as to the effect of the rules, and as to annulment by the resolution of either House of Parliament, as those in the Patents, Designs, and Trade Marks Act, 1883, referred to above.

The Small Holdings and Allotments Act, 1908, made provision for the compulsory purchase or hiring of land by local authorities for the purposes of the Act by an order to be confirmed by the Board of Agriculture and Fisheries, and it provided that an order when so confirmed should become final and have effect as if enacted in the Act, and that the confirmation by the Board should be conclusive evidence that the requirements of the Act had been complied with, and that the order had been duly made and was within the powers of the Act. This latter provision, which effectively ousts the jurisdiction of the Courts to inquire into the validity of any such order, has, as will be seen, found its way into many other statutes providing for the acquisition of land compulsorily. All questions of disputed compensation or rent to be paid for land compulsorily purchased or hired were to be determined by a single arbitrator or valuer appointed by the Board.

The Housing, Town Planning, etc., Act, 1909, by section 17 provided for appeals to the Local Government Board against orders for the closing of dwelling-houses made by local authorities; and by section 39 the procedure on any such appeal was to be such as the Board might by rules determine, and the Board were empowered to make such order in the matter as they thought equitable, the order to be binding and conclusive on all parties, with a *proviso* that the Board should, if so directed by the High Court, state a case for the opinion of the Court on any question of law arising, and that the Board should not dismiss any appeal without having first held a public local inquiry. These provisions, and the duties of the Board in reference to such appeals, were considered in the case of the *Local Government Board* v. *Arlidge*.

The First Schedule to this Act contains provisions for the compulsory purchase of land by local authorities which are in all respects (including the provision as to conclusive evidence) similar to those in the Small Holdings and Allotments Act, 1908, above referred to, with the substitution of the Local Government Board for the Board of Agriculture and Fisheries.

The Trade Boards Act, 1918, gives power to the Minister of Labour by special order to extend or limit the scope of the Trade Boards Act, 1909 (an Act for the regulation of wages in particular trades), every such special order without confirmation by Parliament to have effect as if enacted in the Act, but to be laid before Parliament and to be subject to annulment on the presentation of an address to His Majesty by either House. Before any such order is made, the draft order must be published and a public inquiry be held by a person not in the employment of any Government department, who is to report to the Minister on the draft order.

The Education Act, 1918, provides for the compulsory purchase of land by local education authorities, and for this purpose incorporates the provisions of the First Schedule to the Housing, Town Planning, etc., Act, 1909, above referred to, with the substitution of the Board of Education for the Local Government Board.

Power is given to the Board of Agriculture and Fisheries by the Animals (Anaesthetics) Act, 1919, to extend or vary the provisions of the Act by order, the draft of any such order to be published for a period of three months before the order is made, and the Board to consider any representations by persons interested. An order under the Act does not take effect until it has lain for thirty days on which the House has sat, before each House of Parliament, and during that period is subject to annulment by resolution of either House.

By the Electricity (Supply) Act, 1919, the Electricity Commissioners are given power to formulate schemes for the improvement of the organization for the supply of electricity in any district, and, after holding a local inquiry, to make an order giving effect to any such scheme, and present it for confirmation to the Board of Trade (now the Ministry of Transport), who may confirm it, with or without modification. When confirmed, the order must be laid before each House of Parliament, and does not come into operation until it has been approved, with or without modification, by a resolution passed by each House, but when so approved it has effect as if enacted in the Act. These provisions were considered by the Court of Appeal in the case of *Rex* v. *Electricity Commissioners*, and a writ of prohibition was granted prohibiting the Commissioners from proceeding with the consideration of a scheme which the Court held to be *ultra vires*.

The Gas Regulation Act, 1920, empowers the Board of Trade by order to repeal any enactment requiring gas undertakers to supply gas of any particular illuminating or calorific value, and to modify any statutory or other provision affecting the charges which may be made by the undertakers, any such order to have effect as if enacted in the Act. Orders made in pursuance of these provisions are not required to be laid before Parliament.

Very wide powers to make regulations for carrying the Act into effect are given to the Minister of Labour by the Unemployment Insurance Act, 1920. Such regulations have to be laid before Parliament, and are liable to be annulled on the presentation of an address to His Majesty by either House within twenty days. Subject to this provision, they have effect as if enacted in the Act, and the requirements of section 1 of the Rules Publication Act, 1893 (requiring notices to be given of a proposal to make regulations), are expressly dispensed with. The Act also gave a temporary power to the Minister, in case any difficulty arose in bringing the Act into operation, by order to do anything appearing to him necessary or expedient to bring the Act into operation, and by any such order to modify the provisions of the Act so far as might appear necessary or expedient for carrying the order into effect.

The Roads Act, 1920, provides, by section 9, for an appeal to the Minister of Transport against a refusal by the county council to issue a general licence under the section to a manufacturer of or dealer in vehicles, the Minister having power, on such an appeal, to make any order he thinks just, and such order to be final and not subject to appeal to any Court. The Minister also has power, under section 10 of the Act, to suspend, modify, or determine the liability of any persons, whether by virtue of any Act or otherwise, to pay any sum by way of mileage charges or other annual payments in respect of the use of any road by their vehicles. By section 12 very wide powers of making regulations for carrying the Act into effect are given to the Minister, such regulations to be laid before Parliament, and to be subject to annulment on an address to His Majesty within twenty-one days from either House. Failure to comply with any such regulation renders the offending party liable, on summary conviction, to a penalty of £20. By section 14 of the Act an appeal lies to the Minister against a refusal by any licensing authority to grant a licence to ply for hire with an omnibus, the Minister having power on such an appeal to make such order as he thinks fit, the order being final and not subject to appeal to any Court.

By the Celluloid and Cinematograph Film Act, 1922, the Secretary of State has power by order to modify or add to the regulations set out in the First Schedule to the Act. Orders under this Act are not required to be laid before Parliament.

The Salmon and Freshwater Fisheries Act, 1923, provides for the compulsory purchase or hiring by fishery boards of any fishery, by an order confirmed by the Minister of Agriculture and Fisheries. Such an order, when so confirmed, becomes final and has effect as if enacted in the Act, and the confirmation by the Minister is conclusive evidence that the requirements of the Act have been complied with, and that the order has been duly made and is within the powers of the Act.

Extensive powers of making regulations are given to the Minister of Transport by the London Traffic Act, 1924. Section 10 provides for the making of regulations under twenty-three heads for the purpose of relieving congestion and facilitating traffic in and near London, and these regulations may provide for the suspension or modification of any provisions of any statutes, by-laws, or regulations dealing with the same subject-matter, and may provide for the imposition of fines, recoverable summarily, for breaches thereof; and the making of any regulations under this section is conclusive evidence that the requirements of the section have been complied with. The regulations must be laid before Parliament and may be annulled within twenty-eight days on an address to His Majesty by either House.

The Housing Act, 1925, by sections 11 and 14, provides for appeals to the Ministry of Health against closing or demolition orders made by local authorities. (As to these appeals see the case of the *Local Government Board* v. *Arlidge*.) By section 40 (5) of the Act, an order of the Minister confirming an improvement or reconstruction scheme, when made, has effect as if enacted in the Act. It is not required that such an order should be laid before Parliament. The Third Schedule of this Act provides for the compulsory purchase of land by local authorities for the purposes of Part III. of the Act (*i.e.* for the provision of houses for the working classes). The provisions of this Schedule are similar to those contained in the Small Holdings and Allotments Act, 1907, above referred to.

Under the Town Planning Act, 1925, a town planning scheme, when approved by order of the Minister of Health, has effect as if it were enacted in the Act, and such an order is not required to be laid before Parliament. The Third Schedule of this Act also contains provisions for the compulsory purchase of land by local authorities similar to those contained in the Small Holdings and Allotments Act, 1907.

Section 67 of the Rating and Valuation Act, 1925, provided that if any difficulty arose in bringing into operation any of the provisions of the Act, the Minister of Health might by order remove the difficulty and do anything which appeared to him necessary for bringing such provisions into operation, and any such order might modify the provisions of the Act so far as might appear necessary or expedient for carrying the order into effect. The powers given by this section expired on the 31st March 1929.

The Fertilisers and Feeding Stuffs Act, 1926, empowers the Minister of Agriculture and Fisheries and the Board of Agriculture for Scotland jointly to make regulations generally for carrying the Act into operation, and such regulations may vary any of the Schedules, and thus extend or limit the scope, of the Act. The regulations have to be laid before Parliament, and are subject to annulment on an address to His Majesty from either House within twenty-one days.

Section 211 of the Poor Law Act, 1927, gives very extensive powers to the Minister of Health to make such rules, orders, and regulations as he thinks fit for the management of the poor, the government of workhouses, etc., etc., etc., and generally for carrying the Act into execution in all respects. All rules, orders, and regulations made by the Minister under these powers have effect as if enacted in the Act, subject to the power of the Minister to suspend, alter, or rescind any such rule, order, or regulation. There is no provision requiring that any of such rules, orders, or regulations should be laid before Parliament.

The Road Transport Lighting Act, 1927, gives power to the Minister of Transport by regulations to add to, or vary, the requirements of the Act. Such regulations are required to be laid before Parliament, and are subject to annulment on an address to His Majesty from either House within twenty-eight days.

Patents, Designs, and Trade Marks Act, 1883
(46 & 47 Vict. c. 57)

Section 101. (1) The Board of Trade may from time to time make such general rules and do such things as they think expedient, subject to the provisions of this Act:

(*a*) For regulating the practice of registration under this Act;
(*b*) For classifying goods for the purposes of designs and trade marks;
(*c*) For making or requiring duplicates of specifications, amendments, drawings, and other documents;
(*d*) For securing and regulating the publishing and selling of copies, at such prices and in such manner as the Board of Trade think fit, of specifications, drawings, amendments, and other documents;
(*e*) For securing and regulating the making, printing, publishing, and selling of indexes to, and abridgments of, specifications and other documents in the patent office; and providing for the inspection of indexes and abridgments and other documents;
(*f*) For regulating (with the approval of the Treasury) the presentation of copies of patent office publications to patentees and to public authorities, bodies, and institutions at home and abroad;
(*g*) Generally for regulating the business of the patent office, and all things by this Act placed under the direction or control of the comptroller, or of the Board of Trade.

(2) Any of the forms in the First Schedule to this Act may be altered or amended by rules made by the Board as aforesaid.

(3) General rules may be made under this section at any time after the passing of this Act, but not so as to take effect before the commencement of this Act, and shall (subject as hereinafter mentioned) be of the same effect as if they were contained in this Act, and shall be judicially noticed.

(4) Any rules made in pursuance of this section shall be laid before both Houses of Parliament, if Parliament be in session at the time of making thereof, or, if not, then as soon as practicable after the beginning of the next session of Parliament, and they shall also be advertised twice in the official journal to be issued by the comptroller.

(5) If either House of Parliament, within the next forty days after any rules have been so laid before such House, resolves that such rules or any of them ought to be annulled, the same shall after the date of such resolution be of no effect, without prejudice to the validity of anything done in the meantime under such rules or rule or to the making of any new rules or rule.

LOCAL GOVERNMENT ACT, 1888 (51 & 52 Vict. c. 41)

Section 108. (1) If from any cause there is no returning officer able to act in any county at the first election of a county council, or no register of electors properly made up, or no proper election takes place, or an election of an insufficient number of persons takes place, or any difficulty arises as respects the holding of the first election of county councillors, or as to the first meeting of a provisional council, the Local Government Board may by order appoint a returning officer or other officer, and do any matter of thing which appears to them necessary for the proper holding of the first election, and for the proper holding of the first meeting of the provisional council, and may, if it appears to them necessary, direct a new election to be held, and fix the dates requisite for such new election. Any such order may modify the provisions of this Act and the enactments applied by this Act so far as may appear to the Board necessary for the proper holding of the first election and first meeting of the provisional council.

. . . . . .

(3) The Local Government Board, on the application of a county council or provisional council, may within six months after the day fixed for the first election of the councillors of such council, from time to time, make such orders as appear to them necessary for bringing this Act into full operation as respects the council so applying, and such orders may modify any enactment in this or any other Act, whether general or local and personal, so far as may appear to the Board necessary for the said purpose.

EDUCATION ACT, 1902 (2 Ed. VII. c. 42)

Section 7. (1) The local education authority shall maintain and keep efficient all public elementary schools within their area which are necessary, and have the control of all expenditure required for that purpose, other than expenditure for which, under this Act, provision is to be made by the managers; but, in the case of a school not provided by them, only so long as the following conditions and provisions are complied with:

(*a*) The managers of the school shall carry out any directions of the local education authority as to the secular instruction to be given in the school, including any direction with respect to the number and educational qualifications of the teachers to be employed for such instruction, and for the dismissal of any teacher on educational grounds; and, if the managers fail to carry out any such direction, the local education authority shall, in addition to their other powers, have the power themselves to carry out the direction in question as if they were the managers; but no direction given under this provision shall be such as to interfere with reasonable facilities for religious instruction during school hours;

(*b*) The local education authority shall have power to inspect the school;

(*c*) The consent of the local education authority shall be required to the appointment of teachers, but that consent shall not be withheld except on educational grounds, and the consent of the authority shall also be required to the dismissal of a teacher, unless the dismissal be on grounds connected with the giving of religious instruction in the school;

(*d*) The managers of the school shall provide the school-house free of any charge, except for the teacher's dwelling-house (if any), to the local education authority for use as a public elementary school, and shall out of funds provided by them, keep the school-house in good repair, and make such alterations and improvements in the buildings as may be reasonably required by the local education authority. Provided that such damage as the local authority consider to be due to fair wear and tear in the use of any room in the school-house for the purpose of a public elementary school shall be made good by the local education authority;

(*e*) The managers of the school shall, if the local education authority have no suitable accommodation in schools provided by them, allow that authority to use any room in the school-house out of school hours free of charge for any educational purpose, but this obligation shall not extend to more than three days in the week.

. . . . . .

(3) If any question arises under this section between the local education authority and the managers of a school not provided by the authority, that question shall be determined by the Board of Education.

. . . . . .

Section 16. If the local education authority fail to fulfil any of their duties under the Elementary Education Acts, 1870–1900, or this Act, or fail to provide such additional public school accommodation within the meaning of the Elementary Education Act, 1870, as is, in the opinion of the Board of Education, necessary in any part of their area, the Board of Education may, after holding a public inquiry, make such order as they think necessary or proper for the purpose of compelling the authority to fulfil their duty, and any such order may be enforced by mandamus.

Trade Marks Act, 1905 (5 Ed. VII. c. 15)

Section 60. (1) Subject to the provisions of this Act the Board of Trade may from time to time make such rules, prescribe such forms, and generally do such things as they think expedient:

(*a*) For regulating the practice under this Act;

(*b*) For classifying goods for the purposes of registration of trade marks;

(*c*) For making or requiring duplicates of trade marks and other documents;

(*d*) For securing and regulating the publishing and selling or distributing in such manner as the Board of Trade think fit, of copies of trade marks and other documents;

(*e*) Generally, for regulating the business of the office in relation to trade marks and all things by this Act placed under the direction or control of the Registrar, or of the Board of Trade.

(2) Rules under this section shall, whilst in force, be of the same effect as if they were contained in this Act.

(3) Before making any rules under this section the Board of Trade shall publish notice of their intention to make the rules and of the place where copies of the draft rules may be obtained in such manner as the Board consider most expedient, so as to enable persons affected to make representations to the Board before the rules are finally settled.

(4) Any rules made in pursuance of this section shall be forthwith advertised twice in the *Trade Marks Journal*, and shall be laid before both Houses of Parliament, if Parliament be in session at the time of making thereof, or, if not, then as soon as practicable after the beginning of the then next session of Parliament.

(5) If either House of Parliament within the next forty days after any rules have been so laid before such House, resolve that such rules or any of them ought to be annulled, the same shall after the date of such resolution be of no

effect, without prejudice to the validity of anything done in the meantime under such rules or rule or to the making of any new rules or rule.

PATENTS AND DESIGNS ACT, 1907 (7 Ed. VII. c. 29)

Sect. 86. (1) The Board of Trade may make such general rules and do such things as they think expedient, subject to the provisions of this Act :

(*a*) For regulating the practice of registration under this Act;
(*b*) For classifying goods for the purposes of designs;
(*c*) For making or requiring duplicates of specifications, drawings, and other documents;
(*d*) For securing and regulating the publishing and selling of copies, at such prices and in such manner as the Board of Trade think fit, of specifications, drawings, and other documents;
(*e*) For securing and regulating the making, printing, publishing, and selling of indexes to, and abridgments of, specifications and other documents in the Patent Office, and providing for the inspection of indexes and abridgments and other documents;
(*f*) For regulating (with the approval of the Treasury) the presentation of copies of Patent Office publications to patentees, and to public authorities, bodies, and institutions at home and abroad;
(*g*) For regulating the keeping of the register of patent agents under this Act;
(*h*) Generally for regulating the business of the Patent Office, and all things by this Act placed under the direction or control of the comptroller, or of the Board of Trade.

(2) General rules shall, whilst in force, be of the same effect as if they were contained in this Act.

(3) Any rules made in pursuance of this section shall be advertised twice in the official journal to be issued by the comptroller, and shall be laid before both Houses of Parliament as soon as practicable after they are made, and if either House of Parliament, within the next forty days after any rules have been so laid before that House, resolves that the rules or any of them ought to be annulled, the rules or those to which the resolution applies shall after the date of such resolution be of no effect, without prejudice to the validity of anything done in the meantime under the rules, or to the making of any new rules.

Small Holdings and Allotments Act, 1908
(8 Ed. VII. c. 36)

Sect. 39. (1) Where a council (county, borough, urban district, or parish council) propose to purchase land compulsorily under this Act, the council may, subject to the provisions of Part I. of the First Schedule to this Act, submit to the Board (of Agriculture and Fisheries) an order putting in force as respects the land specified in the order, the provisions of the Lands Clauses Acts with respect to the purchase and taking of land otherwise than by agreement.

(2) Where a council propose to hire land compulsorily, the council may submit to the Board an order for the compulsory hiring of the land specified in the order for a period not less than fourteen nor more than thirty-five years, and the provisions of Part I. of the First Schedule to this Act

shall apply to the order in like manner as it applies to an order for compulsory purchase, with the substitution of "hiring" for "purchase", and with the modification set out in Part II. of the Schedule.

(3) An order under this section shall be of no force unless and until it is confirmed by the Board, and the Board may, subject to the provisions of the First Schedule to this Act, confirm the order either without modification or subject to such modifications as they think fit, and an order when so confirmed shall become final and have effect as if enacted in this Act; and the confirmation by the Board shall be conclusive evidence that the requirements of this Act have been complied with, and that the order has been duly made and is within the powers of this Act.

. . . . . .

(5) In determining the amount of any disputed compensation under any such order, no additional allowance shall be made on account of the purchase or hiring being compulsory.

First Schedule

Part I

(1) The order shall be in the prescribed form, and shall contain such provisions as the Board may prescribe for the purpose of carrying the order into effect, and of protecting the council and the persons interested in the land, and shall incorporate, subject to the necessary adaptations, the Lands Clauses Acts and sections seventy-seven to eighty-five of the Railway Clauses Consolidation Act, 1845, but subject to this modification, that any question of

disputed compensation shall be determined by a single arbitrator appointed by the Board, who shall be deemed to be an arbitrator within the meaning of the Lands Clauses Acts, and the provisions of those Acts with respect to arbitration shall, subject to the provisions of this schedule, apply accordingly.

. . . . . .

Part II

(3) The determination of—

(*a*) The amount of the rent to be paid by the council for the land compulsorily hired;
(*b*) The amount of any other compensation to be paid by the council to any person entitled thereto in respect of the land or any interest therein, or in respect of improvements executed on the land or otherwise; and
(*c*) Where part only of a holding held for an unexpired term is hired, the rent to be paid for the residue of the holding during the remainder of that term;

shall in default of agreement be by valuation by a single valuer appointed by the Board: Provided that, if the land hired is in occupation of a tenant, he may, by notice in writing served on the council before the determination of his tenancy, require that any claims by him against the council which, under the Agriculture Holdings Act, 1908, might be referred to arbitration under that Act, shall be so referred, and in such case those claims shall be determined by arbitration under that Act and not by valuation under this Act.

. . . . . .

Housing, Town Planning, etc., Act, 1909
(9 Ed. VII. c. 44)

Sect. 17. (1) It shall be the duty of every local authority . . . to cause to be made from time to time inspection of their district, with a view to ascertain whether any dwelling-house therein is in a state so dangerous or injurious to health as to be unfit for human habitation, and for that purpose it shall be the duty of the local authority, and of every officer of the local authority, to comply with such regulations and to keep such records as may be prescribed by the (Local Government) Board.

(2) If, on the representation of the medical officer of health, or of any other officer of the authority, or other information given, any dwelling-house appears to them to be in such a state, it shall be their duty to make an order prohibiting the use of the dwelling-house for human habitation (in this Act referred to as a closing order) until in the judgement of the local authority the dwelling-house is rendered fit for that purpose.

(3) Notice of a closing order shall be forthwith served on every owner of the dwelling-house in respect of which it is made, and any owner aggrieved by the order may appeal to the Local Government Board by giving notice of appeal to the Board within fourteen days after the order is served upon him.

. . . . . .

(6) The local authority shall determine any closing order made by them if they are satisfied that the dwelling-house, in respect of which the order has been made, has been rendered fit for human habitation. If on the application of

any owner of a dwelling-house, the local authority refuse to determine a closing order, the owner may appeal to the Local Government Board by giving notice of appeal to the Board within fourteen days after the application is refused.

. . . . . .

Sect. 39. (1) The procedure on any appeal under this Part of this Act, including costs, to the Local Government Board shall be such as the Board may by rules determine, and on any such appeal the Board may make such order in the matter as they think equitable, and any order so made shall be binding and conclusive on all parties, and, where the appeal is against any notice, order, or apportionment given or made by the local authority, the notice, order, or apportionment may be confirmed, varied, or quashed, as the Board think just.

Provided that—

(*a*) The Local Government Board may at any stage of the proceeding or appeal, and shall, if so directed by the High Court, state in the form of a special case for the opinion of the Court any question of law arising in the course of the appeal; and

(*b*) the rules shall provide that the Local Government Board shall not dismiss any appeal without having first held a public local inquiry.

. . . . . .

First Schedule

(1) Where a local authority propose to purchase land compulsorily under this Act, the local authority may submit to the Board an order putting in force as respects the land specified in the order the provisions of the Lands

Clauses Acts with respect to the purchase and taking of land otherwise than by agreement.

(2) An order under this schedule shall be of no force unless and until it is confirmed by the Board, and the Board may confirm the order either without modification or subject to such modification as they think fit, and an order when so confirmed shall, save as otherwise expressly provided by this schedule, become final and have effect as if enacted in this Act; and the confirmation by the Board shall be conclusive evidence that the requirements of this Act have been complied with, and that the order has been duly made and is within the powers of this Act.

(3) In determining the amount of any disputed compensation under any such order, no additional allowance shall be made on account of the purchase being compulsory.

(4) The order shall be in the prescribed form, and shall contain such provisions as the Board may prescribe for the purpose of carrying the order into effect, and of protecting the local authority and the persons interested in the land, and shall incorporate, subject to the necessary adaptations, the Lands Clauses Acts (except section 127 of the Lands Clauses Consolidation Act, 1845) and sections 77 to 85 of the Railways Clauses Consolidation Act, 1845, but subject to this modification, that any question of disputed compensation shall be determined by a single arbitrator appointed by the Board, who shall be deemed to be an arbitrator within the meaning of the Lands Clauses Acts, and the provisions of those Acts with respect to arbitration shall, subject to the provisions of this schedule, apply accordingly.

EXAMPLES FROM STATUTES

TRADE BOARDS ACT, 1918 (8 & 9 Geo. V. c. 32)

Section 1. (1) The Trade Boards Act, 1909 (in this Act referred to as "the principal Act"), shall apply to the trades specified in the Schedule to this Act and to any other trades to which it has been applied by a provisional order made under section one of that Act or by a special order made under this Act by the Minister of Labour (in this Act referred to as "a special order").

(2) The Minister of Labour (in this Act referred to as "the Minister") may make a special order applying the principal Act to any specified trade to which it does not at the time apply if he is of opinion that no adequate machinery exists for the effective regulation of wages throughout the trade, and that accordingly, having regard to the rates of wages prevailing in the trade, or any part of the trade, it is expedient that the principal Act should apply to that trade.

(3) If at any time the Minister is of opinion that the conditions of employment in any trade to which the principal Act applies have been so altered as to render the application of the principal Act to the trade unnecessary, he may make a special order withdrawing that trade from the operation of the principal Act.

(4) If the Minister is of opinion that it is desirable to alter or amend the description of any of the trades specified in the Schedule to the principal Act, he may make a special order altering or amending the said Schedule accordingly.

(5) Any Act confirming a provisional order made in

pursuance of section 1 of the principal Act may be repealed or varied by a special order.

. . . . . .

Section 2. (1) Every special order shall without confirmation by Parliament have effect as if enacted in this Act and may be varied or revoked by a subsequent special order.

(2) The provisions contained in the First Schedule to this Act shall have effect with respect to the procedure for making special orders.

(3) Where the Minister makes any special order he shall publish it in such manner as he thinks best adapted for bringing it to the notice of all persons affected thereby, and the order shall come into operation on the date on which it is so published or on such later date as is specified in that behalf in the order.

(4) Every special order shall be laid before each House of Parliament forthwith, and if an address is presented to His Majesty by either House within the next subsequent forty days on which that House has sat after the order has been so laid, praying that the order may be annulled, His Majesty may annul the order, and it shall thenceforth be void, but without prejudice to the validity of anything previously done thereunder or to the power of making a fresh order.

First Schedule

. . . . . .

(6) The Minister may appoint a competent person not in the employment of any Government Department to

hold an inquiry with regard to any draft order, and to report to him thereon.

(7) The inquiry shall be held in public, and such officer of the Ministry of Labour as is appointed by the Minister in that behalf, and any objector or other person who appears to the person holding the inquiry to be effected, may appear at the inquiry either in person or by counsel, solicitor, or agent.

(8) The witnesses at the inquiry may, if the person holding it thinks fit, be examined on oath.

(9) Subject as aforesaid, the inquiry and all proceedings preliminary and incidental thereto shall be conducted in accordance with regulations made by the Minister.

. . . . . .

EDUCATION ACT, 1918 (8 & 9 Geo. V. c. 39)

Section 34. (1) A local education authority may be authorized to purchase land compulsorily for the purpose of any of their powers or duties under the Education Acts, by means of an order submitted to the Board of Education and confirmed by the Board in accordance with the provisions contained in paragraphs (1) to (13) of the First Schedule to the Housing, Town Planning, etc., Act, 1909, and those provisions shall have effect for the purpose, with the substitution of the Board of Education for the Local Government Board, of the local education authority for the local authority, and of references to the Education Acts for references to "this Act":

. . . . . .

MINISTRY OF TRANSPORT ACT, 1919 (9 & 10 Geo. V. c. 50)

Section 11. An appeal shall lie to the Minister (of Transport) in respect of any restriction upon any traffic passing over or seeking to cross any bridge or culvert, and the Minister shall have power, notwithstanding any provision in any other statute, to make such order as he may think fit concerning the strengthening, standard of maintenance, and maintenance of any bridge or culvert, the traffic using it or seeking to use it, and apportionment of any expenditure involved, but no order made by the Minister under this section shall enlarge the pecuniary liability of any railway or canal company or impose any new liability on any such company.

Section 29. (1) The Minister may make rules in relation to matters preliminary to the making of orders and Orders in Council under this Act which authorize the acquisition of land or easements, or the breaking up of roads and the construction of works, including the publication of notices and advertisements, and the deposit of plans and sections and books of reference to those plans, and the manner in which and the time within which representations or objections are to be made, and to the holding of local inquiries.

Any rules so made shall be laid before Parliament as soon as they are made and shall have the same effect as if enacted in this Act: Provided that, if an Address is presented to His Majesty by either House of Parliament within twenty-one days on which that House has sat next after any such rules are so laid praying that any such rule may be annulled, His Majesty may annul the rule, and it shall thenceforth be void, but without prejudice to the validity of anything done thereunder.

ANIMALS (ANAESTHETICS) ACT, 1919
(9 & 10 Geo. V. c. 54)

Section 3. (1) The Board of Agriculture and Fisheries may, by order made subject to the provisions of this section, add any other operation to the operations specified in any Schedule to this Act, and any operation so added shall be deemed to be an operation specified in that Schedule, and may transfer an operation from one Schedule to another, and the Board of Agriculture and Fisheries may also, by order made as aforesaid, extend any provision of this Act to any domestic animal to which it does not at the time apply, with such modifications or additions as may appear to that Board to be necessary. The Board may, by order made subject to the provisions of this section, declare any substance to be a suitable general anaesthetic or a suitable local anaesthetic for the purposes of this Act, and any substance so declared shall be deemed to be a general anaesthetic or local anaesthetic, as the case may be, of sufficient power to prevent the animal feeling pain if properly applied.

(2) The draft of any such order shall be published for a period of three months before the order is made, and the Board of Agriculture and Fisheries during that period shall receive and consider any representations made to them with respect to the order by any persons appearing to them to be interested in the subject of the order.

(3) The order, when made, shall forthwith be laid before Parliament, and shall not take effect until it has so lain for thirty days before each House of Parliament, being days upon which that House has sat, and if a resolution is passed by either House before the expiration of such days declaring that the order be annulled, the order shall not take effect, but if no such resolution is passed the order shall take effect on such day after the expiration of the last day on which any such resolution might have been passed as the Board of Agriculture and Fisheries may appoint.

Housing (Additional Powers) Act, 1919
(9 & 10 Geo. V. c. 99)

Section 5. (1) Where it appears to a local authority that the provision of dwelling accommodation for their area is or is likely to be delayed by a deficiency of labour or materials arising out of the employment of labour or material in the construction within their area of any works or buildings (other than works or buildings authorized or required by, under, or in pursuance of any Act of Parliament), and that the construction of those works or buildings is in the circumstances of the case of less public importance for the time being than the provision of dwelling accommodation, the authority may by order prohibit for such time and on such terms and subject to such conditions as the Minister (of Health) may from time to time prescribe, and either in whole or in part, the construction of those works or buildings.

(2) Any person aggrieved by an order made by a local authority under this section may, subject to rules of pro-

cedure to be made by the Minister, appeal to the Minister, and on any such appeal the Minister shall refer all such cases to a standing tribunal of appeal, consisting of five persons, to be appointed by the Minister, which shall have power either to annul the order or to make such order in the matter as the local authority could have made, and the decision of the tribunal of appeal in the matter shall be final and not subject to appeal to or review by any Court.

. . . . . .

(4) If any person acts in contravention of or fails to comply with any of the provisions of an order made under this section, he shall be liable on summary conviction to a fine not exceeding one hundred pounds, and, if the offence is a continuing offence, to a fine not exceeding fifty pounds for each day during which the offence continues, and, where the person guilty of an offence under this section is a company, every director and officer of the company shall be guilty of the like offence unless he proves that the act constituting the offence took place without his consent or connivance.

. . . . . .

Section 6. (1) If any person at any time after the third day of December, 1919, without the permission in writing of the local authority within whose area the house is situate, demolishes, in whole or in part, or uses otherwise than as a dwelling-house any house which was at that date in the opinion of the local authority reasonably fit or reasonably capable without reconstruction of being rendered fit for human habitation, he shall be liable on summary conviction in respect of each house demolished or so used to a fine not exceeding one hundred pounds or to imprisonment for a term not exceeding three months or to both such imprisonment and fine, and, where the person guilty of an offence under this section is a company, every director and officer of the company shall be guilty of the like offence unless he proves that the act constituting the offence took place without his consent or connivance.

(2) Any person to whom permission to demolish a house has been refused by a local authority under this section may appeal to the Minister on the ground that the house is not capable without reconstruction of being rendered fit for human habitation, and any such appeal shall be dealt with in the same manner as an appeal under sub-section (2) of the preceding section of this Act.

. . . . . .

ELECTRICITY (SUPPLY) ACT, 1919 (9 & 10 Geo. V. c. 100)

Section 5. (1) The Electricity Commissioners may provisionally determine that any district in the United Kingdom shall be constituted a separate electricity district for the purposes of this Act, and, in considering what areas are to be included in a district, areas shall be grouped in such manner as may seem to the Commissioners most conducive to the efficiency and economy of the supply of electricity and to convenience of administration. Before finally determining the area of any such district, the Electricity Commissioners shall publish notice of their intention so to do and of the area proposed to be included in such district, and shall also give notice thereof to all county councils, local authorities and authorized undertakers any part of whose county district or area of supply is proposed to be included in the electricity district, and, if any objection or representation be made on account of the inclusion in or the exclusion from the proposed district of any area, the Electricity Commissioners shall hold a local inquiry with reference to the area to be included in the proposed district:

Provided that, where a local inquiry is held as hereinafter provided regarding the improvement of the organization of the supply of electricity in any district, the area of that district shall not be finally determined until after that inquiry has been held.

(2) Where it appears to the Electricity Commissioners with respect to any electricity district so provisionally determined that the existing organization for the supply of electricity therein should be improved, the Commissioners shall give notice of their intention to hold a local inquiry into the matter, and shall give to authorized undertakers, county councils, local authorities, railway companies using or proposing to use electricity for traction purposes, large consumers of electricity, and other associations or bodies within the district which appear to the Commissioners to be interested, an opportunity to submit, within such time as the Commissioners may allow, a scheme or schemes for effecting such improvement, including proposals for altering or adjusting the boundaries of the district and, where necessary, the formation of a joint electricity authority for the district.

(3) If no such scheme is submitted within the time

so allowed, or if no scheme submitted is approved by the Commissioners, the Commissioners may themselves formulate such a scheme.

(4) The Electricity Commissioners shall publish, in such manner as they think best adapted for ensuring publicity, any scheme which they have approved, with or without modifications, or which they have themselves formulated, and shall hold a local inquiry thereon.

Section 6. (1) A scheme under the last-foregoing section may provide for the establishment and (where desirable) the incorporation with power to hold land without licence in mortmain, of a joint electricity authority representative of authorized undertakers within the electricity district, either with or without the addition of representatives of the council of any county situate wholly or partly within the electricity district, local authorities, large consumers of electricity, and other interests within the electricity district, and, subject as hereinafter in this Act provided, for the exercise by that authority of all or any of the powers of the authorized undertakers within the electricity district, and for the transfer to the authority of the whole or any part of the undertakings of any of those undertakers, upon such terms as may be provided by the scheme, and the scheme may contain any consequential, incidental, and supplemental provisions which appear to be expedient or proper for the purpose of the scheme, including provisions determining the area included in the electricity district:

Provided that no such scheme shall provide for the transfer to the authority of any part of an undertaking except with the consent of the owners thereof.

(2) The scheme may provide for enabling the joint electricity authority to delegate, with or without restrictions, to committees of the authority any of the powers or duties of the authority, and for the payment out of the revenues of the authority of travelling and subsistence expenses of members of the authority, and reasonable compensation for loss of remunerative time.

Section 7. (1) The Electricity Commissioners may make an order giving effect to the scheme embodying decisions they arrive at as the result of such inquiry as aforesaid, and present the order for confirmation by the Board of Trade, who may confirm the order either without modification or subject to such modifications as they think fit.

(2) Any such order shall be laid, as soon as may be after it is confirmed, before each House of Parliament, but shall not come into operation unless and until it has been approved either with or without modification by a resolution passed by each such House, and when so approved shall have effect as if enacted in this Act.

(3) An order made under this section may be altered by a subsequent order made, confirmed, and approved in like manner as the original order.

. . . . . .

Section 12. (3) Subject to the limitations hereinbefore contained on the powers of a joint electricity authority to supply electricity, the Electricity Commissioners may by order, after such inquiry as they think fit, impose on any joint electricity authority an obligation to supply electricity in such circumstances, within such areas, and on such terms and conditions as to price and otherwise as may be specified in the order.

. . . . . .

Section 34. (1) The Board of Trade and the Electricity Commissioners may respectively make rules in relation to applications and other proceedings before them under this Act, and to the payments to be made in respect thereof, and to the publication of notices and advertisements and the manner in which and the time within which representations or objections with reference to any application or other proceeding are to be made, and to the holding of inquiries in such cases as they may think it advisable, and to the costs of such inquiries, and to any other matters arising in relation to their powers and duties under this Act.

(2) Any rules made in pursuance of this section shall be laid before Parliament as soon as may be after they are made, and shall have the same effect as if enacted in this Act.

Section 35. (1) A special order made under this Act by the Electricity Commissioners shall not have any effect unless and until confirmed by the Board of Trade.

. . . . . .

(3) Before any special order, other than a special order which is not valid unless approved by a resolution passed by each House of Parliament, comes into force it shall be laid before each House of Parliament for a period not less than thirty days during which that House is sitting, and, if either of those Houses before the expiration of those thirty days presents an Address to His Majesty against

the order or any part thereof, no further proceedings shall be taken thereon without prejudice to the making of any new order.

(4) A special order so made and confirmed as aforesaid shall have effect as if enacted in this Act.

GAS REGULATION ACT, 1920 (10 & 11 Geo. V. c. 28)

Section 1. (1) The Board of Trade may, on the application of any gas undertakers, by order, provide for the repeal of any enactment or other provisions requiring the undertakers to supply gas of any particular illuminating or calorific value, and for substituting power to charge for thermal units supplied in the form of gas.

(2) An order under this section may provide for modifying the statutory or other provisions affecting the charges which may be made by the undertakers, by substituting for the standard or maximum price authorized under those provisions a standard or maximum price for each hundred thousand British thermal units (in this Act referred to as "a therm").

. . . . . .

(4) An order made under this section—

(*f*) shall have effect as if enacted in this Act.

. . . . . .

Section 16. (1) The Board of Trade may make rules in relation to applications and other proceedings under this Act and to the payments to be made in respect thereof, and to the publication and services of notices and the publication of advertisements, and the manner in which and the time within which representations or objections with reference to any application or other proceeding are to be made, and to the holding of inquiries in such cases as they may think it advisable and to the costs of such inquiries, and to any other matters arising in relation to their powers and duties under this Act.

(2) Any rules made in pursuance of this section shall be laid before Parliament as soon as may be after they are made and shall have the same effect as if enacted in this Act.

. . . . . .

Section 19. Any provisions of this Act or any order made thereunder shall have effect in lieu of any provisions to the same effect or inconsistent therewith in any Act relating to the testing of gas-measuring instruments, or in any Act or order having the force of an Act relating to an undertaking with respect to which an order has been made under this Act.

Unemployment Insurance Act, 1920
(10 & 11 Geo. V. c. 30)

Section 35. (1) The Minister (of Labour) may make regulations for any of the purposes for which regulations may be made under this Act or the Schedules thereto, and for prescribing anything which under this Act or any such Schedules is to be prescribed, and also—

(*a*) for permitting persons who are engaged under the same employer partly in an occupation employment in which make them employed persons within the meaning of this Act and partly in some other occupation to be treated, with the consent of the employer, for the purposes of this Act, as if they were wholly engaged in the first-mentioned occupation; and

(*b*) for prescribing the evidence to be required as to the fulfilment of the conditions and the absence of the disqualifications for receiving or continuing to receive unemployment benefit, and for that purpose requiring the attendance of insured contributors at such offices or places and at such times as may be required, and requiring employers to answer inquiries relating to any matters on which the fulfilment of the conditions on the absence of the disqualifications depends.

(*c*) for prescribing the manner in which claims for unemployment benefit may be made, the procedure to be followed on the consideration and examination of claims and questions to be considered and determined by the Minister, umpire, insurance officers, and courts of referees, and the mode in which any question may be raised as to the continuance, in the case of a person in receipt of unemployment benefit, of the benefit; and

(*d*) for making provision with respect to the appointment of persons to act in the place of the umpire or any deputy-umpire in the case of the unavoidable absence or incapacity of the umpire or any deputy-umpire; and

(*e*) with respect to the payment of contributions and benefits during any period intervening between any application for the determination of any question or any claim for benefit and the final determination of the question or claim; and

(*f*) for providing in the case of any persons who are insured at the commencement of this Act under the enactments repealed by this Act for the transition from the provisions of those Acts to the provisions of this Act; and

(*g*) generally for carrying this Act into effect.

. . . . . .

(3) All regulations made under this Act shall be laid before each House of Parliament as soon as may be after they are made, and, if an Address is presented to His Majesty by either House of Parliament within the next subsequent twenty days on which that House has sat next after any such regulation is laid before it, praying that the regulation may be annulled, it shall thenceforth be void, but without prejudice to the validity of anything previously done thereunder, or to the making of any new regulation.

(4) Any regulations made under this Act shall have effect as if enacted in this Act.

(5) Section 1 of the Rules Publication Act, 1893 (which required notices to be given of a proposal to make statutory rules), shall not apply to any regulations made under this Act.

. . . . . .

Section 45. If any difficulty arises with respect to the constitution of special or supplementary schemes or otherwise in any manner whatsoever in bringing this Act into operation, the Minister, with the consent of the Treasury, may by order do anything which appears to him necessary or expedient for the constitution of such schemes or for otherwise bringing this Act into operation, and any such order may modify the provisions of this Act so far as may appear necessary or expedient for carrying the order into effect:

Provided that the Minister shall not exercise the powers conferred by this section after one year from the commencement of this Act.

Roads Act, 1920 (10 & 11 Geo. V. c. 72)

Section 9. (1) If any person being a manufacturer of or dealer in vehicles makes, in the prescribed manner, an application in that behalf to the council of the county in which his business premises are situate, that he may be entitled, in lieu of taking out a licence for each vehicle kept by him at the appropriate rate of duty chargeable under the Second Schedule to the Finance Act, 1920, to take out a general licence in respect of all vehicles used by him the council may, subject to the prescribed conditions, issue to him such a licence on payment of duty at the yearly rate of ten pounds, or, in the case of a licence to be used only on vehicles chargeable with duty under paragraph 1 or paragraph 2 of the said Schedule, at the yearly rate of thirty shillings.

. . . . . .

(3) If any person is aggrieved by the refusal of a council to issue a general licence under this section, he may appeal to the Minister (of Transport), and the Minister shall, on any such appeal, make such order in the matter as he thinks just, and the council shall comply with any order so made.

An order made by the Minister under this provision shall be final and not subject to appeal to any Court, and shall, on the application of the Minister, be enforceable by writ of mandamus.

Section 10. Where any persons are, whether by virtue of any Act or otherwise, liable to pay any sums, by way of mileage charges or other annual payments, in respect of the use of any road by their vehicles, the Minister may on an application by those persons in that behalf, and after considering any objections made by any person interested, suspend, modify, or determine the liability to make the payment, as he shall think fit.

. . . . . .

Section 12. (1) The Minister may make regulations generally for the purpose of carrying this Act into effect, and in particular, without prejudice to the generality of the foregoing provision, may make regulations—

(*a*) with respect to the registration of vehicles; and
(*b*) requiring county councils to make the prescribed returns with respect to vehicles registered with them, and for making any particulars contained in the register available for use by the prescribed persons; and
(*c*) prescribing the size, shape, and character of the identification marks or the signs to be fixed on any vehicle and the manner in which those marks or signs are to be displayed and rendered easily distinguishable, whether by night or by day; and
(*d*) requiring any person to whom any vehicle is sold or disposed of to furnish the prescribed particulars in the prescribed manner; and
(*e*) providing for the issue of registration books in respect of the registration of any vehicle, and for the sur-

render and production, and the inspection by the prescribed persons, of any book so issued, and for the issue of new registration books and new licences in the place of any such books or licences which may be lost or destroyed, and for the fee (not exceeding five shillings) to be paid on the issue of a new registration book or licence; and

(*f*) prescribing the form of, and the particulars to be included in, the register with respect to vehicles for which a general licence has been taken out by a manufacturer or dealer and the identification marks to be carried by any such vehicle, and defining the purposes for which the holder of a general licence may use a vehicle or a road; and

(*g*) extending any provisions as to registration, and provisions incidental to any such provisions, to any vehicles in respect of which duty under section 13 of the Finance Act, 1920, is not payable (including vehicles belonging to the Crown), and for providing for the identification of any such vehicle; and

(*h*) prescribing any matter which is to be prescribed under this Act.

(2) Every regulation made under this Act shall be laid before each House of Parliament as soon as may be after it is made, and, if an address is presented to His Majesty within twenty-one days on which that House has sat next after any such regulation is laid before it praying that the regulation may be annulled, His Majesty in Council may annul the regulation, and it shall thenceforth be void, but without prejudice to the validity of anything previously done thereunder.

(3) County councils shall comply with any regulations so made by the Minister under this Act.

(4) If any person acts in contravention of, or fails to comply with, any regulations made under this Act, he shall for each offence be liable on summary conviction to a penalty not exceeding twenty pounds.

Section 14. (3) Where, upon application for a licence to ply for hire with an omnibus, the licensing authority either refuses to grant a licence or grants a licence subject to conditions, in either case the applicant shall have a right of appeal to the Minister of Transport from the decision of the licensing authority, and the Minister shall have power to make such order thereon as he thinks fit, and such order shall be binding upon the licensing authority.

An order made by the Minister under this sub-section shall be final and not subject to appeal to any Court, and shall, on the application of the Minister, be enforceable by writ of mandamus.

For the purpose of this sub-section the expression "omnibus" includes every omnibus, char-a-banc, wagonette, brake, stage-coach, or other carriage plying for hire or used to carry passengers at separate fares.

Celluloid and Cinematograph Film Act, 1922
(12 & 13 Geo. V. c. 35)

Section 1. (4) The Secretary of State may by order made in accordance with the provisions contained in the Second Schedule to this Act—

(*a*) make regulations with respect to the use of any

cinematograph or similar apparatus upon any premises used for any purpose to which this Act applies; and

(*b*) modify or add to the regulations set out in the First Schedule to this Act, and those regulations shall thereupon have effect as so modified or added to.

An order made under this section may apply either generally, or to such classes or descriptions of premises as may be mentioned in the order.

ELECTRICITY SUPPLY ACT, 1922 (12 & 13 Geo. V. c. 46)

Section 14. (1) The Electricity Commissioners by an order establishing a joint electricity authority or a special order may, as regards any undertaking or part of an undertaking of any authorized undertakers, suspend any powers of a joint electricity authority or the London County Council or any local authority relating to the purchase of such undertaking or part thereof for such period and on such conditions (if any) as the Electricity Commissioners may think fit, and may for that purpose amend the provisions of any Act or order relating to such undertaking: Provided that no such powers shall be suspended under the provisions of this section except with the consent of the authority or authorities in whom the said powers are vested.

(2) Where under the powers of this section the Electricity Commissioners suspend any powers of purchase relating to the undertaking of any authorized undertakers or any part thereof, they may make provision as to the relation between the prices which may be charged for electricity and the dividends to be paid by such undertakers.

SALMON AND FRESHWATER FISHERIES ACT, 1923
(13 & 14 Geo. V. c. 16)

Section 16. (3) Where a fishery board propose to purchase an obstruction or fishery compulsorily under this section, the fishery board may, subject to the provisions of Part I. of the First Schedule to this Act, submit to the Minister (of Agriculture and Fisheries) an order putting in force as respects the obstruction or fishery specified in the order the provisions of the Land Clauses Acts with respect to the purchase and taking of land otherwise than by agreement.

(4) Where a fishery board propose to hire an obstruction or fishery compulsorily, the fishery board may submit to the Minister an order for the compulsory hiring of the obstruction or fishery specified in the order for a period not less than fourteen nor more than thirty-five years, and the provisions of Part I. of the First Schedule to this Act shall apply to the order in like manner as it applies to an order for compulsory purchase, with the substitution of "hiring" for "purchase" and with the modifications set out in Part II. of that Schedule.

(5) An order under this section shall be of no force unless and until it is confirmed by the Minister, and the Minister may, subject to the provisions of the First Schedule to this Act, confirm the order either without modification or subject to such modifications as he thinks fit, and an order when so confirmed shall become final and have effect as if enacted in this Act, and the confirmation by the Minister shall be conclusive evidence that the requirements of this

Act have been complied with, and that the order has been duly made and is within the powers of this Act:

Provided that, when the order relates to a dam constructed under any Act of Parliament, the order shall be provisional only and shall not have effect unless and until it is confirmed by Parliament.

London Traffic Act, 1924 (14 & 15 Geo. V. c. 34)

Section 7. (1) Where as respects any street or part of a street within the area consisting of the city of London and the metropolitan police district, the Minister (of Transport) is of opinion that by reason—

(*a*) of the width of the street or part of the street or the density of traffic thereon; or

(*b*) of the existence of alternative facilities for the conveyance of passengers along the street or part of the street or in proximity thereto, or of the omnibus accommodation on the street or part of the street being excessive;

it is desirable that an order under this section shall be made, he may by order declare the street or part of the street to be a street in which the plying for hire by omnibuses ought to be prohibited or restricted either generally or during particular hours, and a street or part of a street with respect to which such an order is made is hereinafter referred to as a "restricted street".

(2) Where the Minister has so declared any street or part of a street to be a restricted street, the Minister may make regulations—

(*a*) prohibiting or restricting the plying for hire by omnibuses in the street either generally or during particular hours, or limiting the aggregate number of journeys which may be made in either direction along the street during particular hours by omnibuses plying for hire;

(*b*) determining the omnibus proprietors whose omnibuses alone may ply for hire on the street and apportioning amongst those proprietors such aggregate number of journeys as aforesaid; but so, nevertheless, that the right so to ply shall not be limited to the omnibuses of one proprietor in any case where it appears to the Minister to be reasonable and practicable that the right should be exercised by other omnibuses also; and

(*c*) conferring on a licensing authority such powers as he may deem necessary to enable them to secure the observance of the regulations; and the

regulations may provide for dispensing with or relaxing the restrictions imposed thereby in such circumstances and in such manner as may be provided in the regulations.

. . . . . .

(4) If any person contravenes or fails to comply with any such regulations, he shall be liable on summary conviction to a fine not exceeding five pounds, and on the conviction of a person for a second or subsequent offence under this sub-section, the licensing authority shall notify the Minister of the conviction and the licensing authority, if so directed by the Minister, shall thereupon revoke or suspend all or any licences to ply for hire in the area aforesaid which they may have granted to the offender in respect of omnibuses:

Provided that proceedings for any such offence shall not be instituted except by or on behalf of a licensing or police authority.

. . . . . .

(6) Any regulations made under this section shall be laid before both Houses of Parliament forthwith; and, if an address is presented to His Majesty by either House of Parliament within the next subsequent twenty-eight days on which that House has sat after any such regulation is laid before it praying that the regulation may be annulled, it shall thenceforth be void, but without prejudice to the validity of anything previously done thereunder or the making of a new regulation.

Section 10. (1) For the purpose of relieving congestion and facilitating traffic in and near London, the Minister may make regulations to have effect in the London Traffic Area, or any such part thereof or places or street therein, as may be specified in the regulations, for any of the purposes or with reference to any of the matters set out in the Third Schedule to this Act, and special regulations applicable only at special times or on special occasions may be so made:

Provided always that no such regulations shall interfere with street markets nor (so far as respects matters which may be dealt with by regulations under section one of the Metropolitan Streets Amendment Act, 1867) with street traders.

(2) Any regulations so made by the Minister may provide for the suspension or modification so long as the regulations remain in force of any provisions of any Acts (whether

public, general, or local or private), bye-laws, or regulations dealing with the same subject-matter as the regulations made by the Minister, or of any Acts conferring power of making bye-laws or regulations dealing with the same subject-matter, so far as such provisions apply to any place or street to which the regulations made by the Minister apply.

(3) Any such regulations may provide for imposing fines recoverable summarily in respect of breaches thereof not exceeding in the case of a first offence twenty pounds, or in the case of a second or subsequent offence fifty pounds, together with, in the case of a continuing offence, a further fine not exceeding five pounds for each day the offence continues after notice of the offence has been given in such manner as may be prescribed by the regulations.

. . . . . .

(6) The making of any regulations under this section shall be conclusive evidence that the requirements of this section have been complied with.

(7) Any regulation under this section shall be laid before both Houses of Parliament forthwith; and, if an address is presented to His Majesty by either House of Parliament within the next subsequent twenty-eight days on which that House has sat after any such regulation is laid before it praying that the regulation may be annulled, it shall thenceforth be void, but without prejudice to the validity of anything previously done thereunder or the making of a new regulation.

Third Schedule

Purposes or matters for or with respect to which regulations may be made by the Minister

(1) For prescribing the routes to be followed by all classes of traffic, or of any particular class or classes of traffic or vehicles, from one specified point to another, either generally or between any specified times.

(2) For prescribing streets which are not to be used for traffic by vehicles of any specified class or classes, either generally or at specified times.

(3) For regulating the relative position in the roadway of traffic of differing speeds or types.

(4) For prescribing the places where vehicles or vehicles of any particular class or description may not turn so as to face in the opposite direction to that in which they were proceeding, or where they may only so turn under conditions prescribed by the regulations.

(5) For prescribing the conditions subject to which, and the times at which, articles of exceptionally heavy weight or exceptionally large dimensions may be carried by road.

(6) For prescribing the number and maximum size and weight of trailers which may be drawn on streets by vehicles, or vehicles of any particular class or description, either generally or on streets of any class or description, and for prescribing that a man should be carried on the trailer or, where more than one trailer is drawn, on the rear trailer for signalling to the driver.

(7) For prescribing the conditions subject to which, and the times at which, articles may be loaded on to or un-

loaded from vehicles, or vehicles of any particular class or description, on streets.

(8) For prescribing the conditions subject to which, and the times at which, vehicles, or vehicles of any particular class or description, delivering or collecting goods or merchandise, or delivering goods or merchandise of any particular class or classes, may stand in streets, or in streets of any class or description, or in specified streets.

(9) For prescribing the conditions subject to which, and the times at which, vehicles, or vehicles of any particular class or description, may be used on streets for collecting refuse.

(10) For prescribing rules as to precedence to be observed as between vehicles proceeding in the same direction, or in opposite directions, or when crossing.

(11) For prescribing the conditions subject to which, and the times at which, horses, cattle, sheep, and other animals may be led or driven on streets within the Metropolitan police district and the City of London.

(12) For requiring the erection, exhibition, and removal of traffic notices, and as to the form, plan, and character of such notices.

(13) Broken down vehicles.

(14) Vehicles, or vehicles of any particular class or description, when unattended.

(15) Places in streets where vehicles, or vehicles of any particular class or description, may, or may not, wait either generally or at particular times.

(16) Cab ranks and ranks and stopping places of omnibuses and other public conveyances.

(17) Cabs and hackney carriages not hired and being in a street elsewhere than on a cab rank.

(18) For restricting the use of vehicles and animals, and of sandwichmen and other persons, in streets for the purposes of advertisement of such a nature or in such a manner as to be likely to be a source of danger or to cause obstruction to traffic.

(19) The lighting and guarding of street works.

(20) The erection or placing or the removal of any works or objects likely to hinder the free circulation of traffic in any street, or likely to occasion danger to passengers or vehicles.

(21) Queues of persons waiting in streets.

(22) Priority of entry to public vehicles.

(23) For enabling any police, local or other public authority, in the event of any person failing to do anything which under the regulations he ought to have done, to do such act, and to recover the expenses thereof from the person so in default summarily as a civil debt.

Housing Act, 1925 (15 Geo. V. c. 14)

Section 11. (1) If, on the representation of the medical officer of health, or of any other officer of a local authority, or on other information given, any dwelling-house appears to the local authority to be in a state so dangerous or injurious to health as to be unfit for human habitation, the local authority shall make a closing order prohibiting the use of the house for human habitation until, in the judgement of the local authority, the house is rendered fit for that purpose.

(2) Notice of a closing order shall be forthwith served on every owner of the house in respect of which it is made, and any owner aggrieved by the order may appeal to the Minister (of Health) by giving notice of appeal to the Minister within fourteen days after the notice is served upon him.

. . . . . .

(5) The local authority shall determine any closing order made by them if they are satisfied that the house, in respect of which the order has been made, has been rendered fit for human habitation.

(6) If, on the application of any owner of a house, the local authority refuse to determine a closing order, the owner may appeal to the Minister by giving notice of appeal to the Minister within fourteen days after the application is refused.

. . . . . .

Section 14. (1) Where a closing order in respect of any dwelling-house has remained operative for a period of three months, the local authority shall take into consideration the question of the demolition of the house, and shall give every owner of the house notice of the time (being some time not less than one month after the service of the notice) and place at which the question will be considered, and any owner of the house shall be entitled to be heard when the question is so taken into consideration.

(2) If upon any such consideration the local authority are of opinion that the house has not been rendered fit for human habitation, and that the necessary steps are not being taken with all due diligence to render it so fit, or

that the continuance of any building, being or being part of the house, is a nuisance or dangerous or injurious to the health of the public or of the inhabitants of the neighbouring houses, they shall order the demolition of the house or building.

(4) Notice of an order for the demolition of a house or building shall be forthwith served on every owner of the house or building in respect of which it is made, and any owner aggrieved by the order may appeal to the Minister by giving notice of appeal to the Minister within twenty-one days after the notice is served upon him, or, where the operation of the order has been postponed for any period, within fourteen days after the expiration of that period.

. . . . . .

Section 39. As soon as an improvement or reconstruction scheme has been prepared the local authority shall forthwith—

(*a*) publish, in a newspaper circulating within the district of the local authority, an advertisement stating the fact of such a scheme having been made, the limits of the area comprised therein, and naming a place within that area or in the vicinity thereof where a copy of the scheme may be seen at all reasonable hours; and

(*b*) serve a notice on every owner or reputed owner, lessee or reputed lessee, and occupier (except tenant for a month or a less period than a month) of any lands proposed to be taken compulsorily so far as such persons can reasonably be ascertained, stating that such lands are proposed to be taken compulsorily for the purpose of such a scheme, and in the case of any owner or reputed owner, lessee or reputed lessee, requiring an answer stating whether the person so served dissents or not in respect of taking such lands.

Section 40. (1) Upon compliance with the foregoing provisions with respect to the publication of an advertisement and the service of notices, the local authority shall present a petition to the Minister praying that an order may be made confirming such scheme.

. . . . . .

(3) The Minister after considering the petition may cause a local inquiry to be held, and, if satisfied on the report thereon that the circumstances are such as to justify the making of the scheme and that the carrying into effect of the scheme, either absolutely or subject to conditions or modifications, would be beneficial to the health of the inhabitants of the area in question or of the neighbouring dwelling-houses, may by order confirm the scheme with or without such conditions or modifications, so however that no addition shall be made to the lands proposed in the scheme to be taken compulsorily.

. . . . . .

(5) The order of the Minister when made shall have effect as if enacted in this Act.

. . . . . .

Section 50. (1) Where an official representation is made to the local authority with a view to their passing a resolution in favour of an improvement scheme, and they fail to pass any resolution in relation to such representation, or pass a resolution to the effect that they will not proceed with such scheme, the local authority shall, as soon as possible, send a copy of the official representation, accompanied by their reasons for not acting upon it, to the Minister, and upon receipt thereof the Minister may direct a local inquiry to be held, and a report to be made to him with respect to the correctness of the official representation made to the local authority, and any matters connected therewith on which the Minister may desire to be informed.

(2) If, on the report made to the Minister on an inquiry directed by him under this section, he is satisfied that a scheme ought to have been made for the improvement of the area to which the inquiry relates, or of some part thereof, he may, if he thinks fit, order the local authority to make either an improvement or a reconstruction scheme as he may think fit, and to do all things necessary under this Act for carrying into execution the scheme so made, and the local authority shall accordingly make a scheme or direct a scheme to be prepared as if they had passed the resolution required under this part of this Act in relation to the scheme in question, and do all things necessary under this Act for carrying the scheme into effect.

(3) Any such order of the Minister may be enforced by mandamus.

Third Schedule

Provisions as to the compulsory acquisition of land by a local authority for the purposes of Part III. of this Act (provision of houses for the working classes).

(1) Where a local authority propose to purchase land compulsorily, the local authority may submit to the Minister an order putting in force as respects the land specified in the order the provisions of the Lands Clauses Acts with

respect to the purchase and taking of land otherwise than by agreement.

(2) An order under this Schedule shall be of no force unless and until it is confirmed by the Minister, and the Minister may confirm the order either without modification or subject to such modifications as he thinks fit, and an order when so confirmed shall, save as otherwise expressly provided by this Schedule, become final and have effect as if enacted in this Act; and the confirmation by the Minister shall be conclusive evidence that the requirements of this Act have been complied with, and that the order has been duly made and is within the powers of this Act.

. . . . . .

TOWN PLANNING ACT, 1925 (15 Geo. V. c. 16)

Section 2. (2) A town planning scheme prepared or adopted by a local authority shall not have effect unless it is approved by order of the Minister (of Health), and the Minister may refuse to approve any scheme except with such modifications and subject to such conditions as he thinks fit to impose.

(3) A town planning scheme, when approved by the Minister, shall have effect as if it were enacted in this Act.

. . . . . .

Section 5. (1) The Minister may prescribe a set of general provisions (or separate sets of general provisions adapted for areas of any special character) for carrying out the general objects of town planning schemes, and in particular for dealing with the matters set out in the First Schedule to this Act, and the general provisions or set of general provisions appropriate to the area, for which a town planning scheme is made, shall take effect as part of every scheme, except so far as provision is made by the scheme as approved by the Minister for the variation or exclusion of any of those provisions.

. . . . . .

Section 6. (1) The Minister may make regulations for regulating generally the procedure to be adopted—

(*a*) with respect to the preparation or adoption of a town planning scheme;
(*b*) with respect to obtaining the approval of the Minister to a scheme so prepared or adopted;
(*c*) with respect to the variation or revocation of a scheme;
(*d*) with respect to any inquiries, reports, notices, or other matters required in connection with the preparation or adoption or the approval of the scheme or preliminary thereto, or in relation to the carrying out of the scheme or enforcing the observance of the provisions thereof, or the variation or revocation of the scheme.

. . . . . .

Section 7. (3) If any question arises whether any building or work contravenes a town planning scheme, or whether any provision of a town planning scheme is not complied with in the erection or carrying out of any such building or works, that question shall be referred to the Minister, and shall, unless the parties otherwise agree, be determined by the Minister as arbitrator, and the decision of the Minister shall be final and conclusive.

. . . . . .

Section 13. (1) Where the Minister is satisfied, after

holding a public local inquiry, that a town planning scheme ought to be made by a local authority as respects any land in regard to which a town planning scheme may be made under this Act, the Minister may by order require the local authority to prepare and submit for his approval such a scheme, and, if the scheme is approved by the Minister, to do all things necessary for enforcing the observance of the scheme or any provisions thereof effectively, and for executing any works which, under the scheme or under this Act, the authority are required to execute.

. . . . . .

Section 14. (1) If the Minister is satisfied on any representation, after holding a public inquiry, that a local authority have failed to adopt any scheme proposed by owners of any land in a case where the scheme ought to be adopted, the Minister may order the local authority to adopt the scheme proposed, or in lieu of making such an order as aforesaid, may approve the proposed scheme, subject to such modifications or conditions, if any, as the Minister thinks fit, and thereupon the scheme shall have effect as if it had been adopted by the local authority and approved by the Minister.

. . . . . .

(3) Any order under this section may be enforced by mandamus.

Third Schedule

Part I.

Provisions as to the compulsory acquisition of land.

(1) Where a local authority propose to purchase land

compulsorily, the local authority may submit to the Minister an order putting in force as respects the land specified in the order the provisions of the Lands Clauses Acts with respect to the purchase and taking of land otherwise than by agreement.

(2) An order under this schedule shall be of no force unless and until it is confirmed by the Minister, and the Minister may confirm the order either without modification or subject to such modifications as he thinks fit, and an order when so confirmed shall, save as otherwise expressly provided by this schedule, become final and have effect as if enacted in this Act; and the confirmation by the Minister shall be conclusive evidence that the requirements of this Act have been complied with, and that the order has been duly made and is within the powers of this Act.

Rating and Valuation Act, 1925
(15 & 16 Geo. V. c. 90)

Section 66. (1) The Minister (of Health) may by order make such adaptations in the provisions of any local Act as may seem to him to be necessary in order to make those provisions conform with the provisions of this Act.

(2) Every order under this section shall be laid before both Houses of Parliament forthwith, and if an Address is presented to His Majesty by either House of Parliament within the next subsequent twenty-eight days on which that House has sat after any such order is laid before it praying that the order may be annulled it shall thenceforth be void, but without prejudice to the validity of any-

thing previously done thereunder or the making of a new order.

Section 67. (1) If any difficulty arises in connection with the application of this Act to any exceptional area, or the preparation of the first valuation list for any area, or otherwise in bringing into operation any of the provisions of this Act, the Minister may by order remove the difficulty or constitute any assessment committee, or declare any assessment committee to be duly constituted, or make any appointment, or do any other thing, which appears to him necessary or expedient for securing the due preparation of the list or for bringing the said provisions into operation, and any such order may modify the provisions of this Act so far as may appear to the Minister necessary or expedient for carrying the order into effect:

Provided that the Minister shall not exercise the powers conferred by this section after the thirty-first day of March, nineteen hundred and twenty-nine.

(2) Every order made under this section shall be laid before both Houses of Parliament forthwith, and if an Address is presented to His Majesty by either House of Parliament within the next subsequent twenty-eight days on which that House has sat after any such order is laid before it praying that the order may be annulled it shall thenceforth be void, but without prejudice to the validity of anything previously done thereunder or the making of a new order.

. . . . . .

EXAMPLES FROM STATUTES

Fertilizers and Feeding Stuffs Act, 1926
(16 & 17 Geo. V. c. 45)

Section 23. (1) The Minister (of Agriculture and Fisheries) and the Board of Agriculture for Scotland jointly may, after consultation with the advisory committee to be constituted under this section, make regulations for prescribing anything which under this Act is required or authorized to be prescribed, and generally for carrying this Act into operation, and in particular such regulations may provide—

(*a*) for varying any of the Schedules to this Act;
(*b*) for prescribing the manner in which articles required to be marked under this Act are to be marked and the nature of such marks;
(*c*) for prescribing the limits of variation for the purposes of this Act;
(*d*) for prescribing the manner in which samples are to be taken and dealt with in cases where under this Act they are taken in the prescribed manner;
(*e*) as to the method in which analyses for determining the percentages of particular substances are to be made;
(*f*) as to the qualifications to be possessed by agricultural analysts and deputy agriculture analysts and as to the form of certificates of analysis given by them;

and where any schedule is varied by regulations so made, this Act shall have effect as if the Schedule as so varied were substituted for the Schedule contained in this Act.

(2) For the purpose of assisting and advising them with respect to the making of regulations under this Act, the Minister and Board shall, after consultation with such

associations as appear to them to represent the interests concerned, jointly appoint an advisory committee.

(3) All regulations made under this section shall be laid before Parliament as soon as may be after they are made, and if either House of Parliament, within the next subsequent twenty-one days on which that House has sat next after the regulations are laid before them, present an Address to His Majesty praying that the regulations or any part of them may be annulled, they shall thenceforth be void, but without prejudice to the validity of anything previously done thereunder or to the making of new regulations.

Note.—The Schedules to the Act deal with the articles to which the provisions of the Act are applicable; ingredients in feeding stuffs the presence of which must be declared; definitions implied on the sale of articles under certain names; and deleterious ingredients in feeding stuffs.

Sale of Food (Weights & Measures) Act, 1926
(16 & 17 Geo. V. c. 63)

Section 9. (1) The Board of Trade, after consultation with the Minister of Agriculture and Fisheries and such interests as appear to them to be concerned, may make regulations for the purpose—

(*a*) of making additions to or removal from or otherwise varying the list of articles set forth in the First Schedule to this Act;

(*b*) of requiring any articles of food other than those

required by this Act to be sold by weight or by measure to be sold only by weight or by measure, and of applying to any such articles any of the provisions of this Act, either without modification or subject to such modifications as may be specified in the regulations;

(*c*) of requiring any pre-packed articles of food other than those mentioned in the First Schedule to this Act to be labelled with an indication of their weight or measure;

(*d*) of prescribing the manner in which indications of weight or measure are to be marked on pre-packed articles required by or under this Act to be marked with such indications, and the manner of resealing wrappers and containers broken open under this Act; and where the First Schedule is varied by the regulations this Act shall have effect as if the Schedule as so varied was substituted for the Schedule contained in this Act.

(2) Before any regulations other than regulations under paragraph (*d*) of sub-section (1) of this section are made, the draft of the proposed regulations shall be laid before both Houses of Parliament, and the regulations shall not be made unless both Houses by resolution approve the draft either without modification or addition or with modifications or additions to which both Houses agree, but upon such approval being given the regulations may be made in the form in which they have been so approved.

Regulations made under paragraph (*d*) of sub-section (1) of this section shall be laid before both Houses of Parliament as soon as may be after they are made.

(3) Regulations made under this section, if and so far as they relate to pre-packed articles, shall not come into

force before the expiration of a period of six months after they are made.

POOR LAW ACT, 1927 (17 & 18 Geo. V. c. 14)

Section 155. (1) Any person aggrieved by any allowance, disallowance, or surcharge, in lieu of making application to the High Court for a writ of certiorari, may apply to the Minister (of Health) to inquire into and decide upon the lawfulness of the reasons stated by the district auditor for the allowance, disallowance, or surcharge, and thereupon the Minister may issue such order therein as he may deem requisite for determining the question.

(2) Where an appeal is made to the Minister against any allowance, disallowance, or surcharge, the Minister may decide the appeal according to the merits of the case, and if he finds that any disallowance or surcharge is or has been lawfully made, but that the subject matter thereof was incurred under such circumstances as to make it fair and equitable that the disallowance or surcharge should be remitted, he may direct it to be remitted upon payment of the costs, if any, which may have been incurred by the district auditor or other competent authority in enforcing the disallowance or surcharge.

Section 211. (1) For executing the powers given to him by this Act the Minister shall make such rules, orders, and regulations as he may think fit for—

(*a*) the management of the poor;

(*b*) the government of workhouses and the education of children therein;

(*c*) the apprenticing of children of poor persons;

(*d*) the guidance and control of boards of guardians and their offices so far as relates to the management or relief of the poor and subject to the provisions of this Act prescribing their duties;

(*e*) the making and entering into contracts in all matters relating to such management or relief, or to any expenditure for the relief of the poor;

(*f*) the keeping, examining, auditing, and allowing of accounts; and

(*g*) any purposes for which rules, orders, and regulations may be made under this Act and generally the carrying of this Act into execution in all other respects.

(2) All rules, orders, and regulations made by the Minister under this Act shall have effect as if enacted in this Act, subject however to the power of the Minister to suspend, alter or rescind any such rule, order, or regulation.

ROAD TRANSPORT LIGHTING ACT, 1927
(17 & 18 Geo. V. c. 37)

Section 1. (1) Subject to the provisions of this Act and of any regulations made thereunder by the Minister of Transport (in this Act referred to as "the Minister") every vehicle on any road shall during the hours of darkness carry—

(*a*) two lamps, each showing to the front a white light visible from a reasonable distance;

(*b*) one lamp showing to the rear a red light visible from a reasonable distance;

and every such lamp shall, while the vehicle is on any road during such hours as aforesaid, be kept properly trimmed, lighted, and in efficient condition, and shall be attached to the vehicle in such position and manner as the Minister may by regulations prescribe.

It shall be the duty of any person who causes or permits a vehicle to be on the road during the hours of darkness to provide the vehicle with lamps in accordance with the requirements of this Act and of any regulations made thereunder.

(2) The Minister shall have power by regulation to exempt either wholly or partially, and subject to such conditions as may be specified in the regulation, from any of the requirements of this Act—

(*a*) any vehicles, or vehicles of any class or description, while carrying inflammable or explosive goods of a nature specified in the regulation, or being in a place where inflammable or explosive material of a nature so specified is handled or stored, if an application is made for the purpose by any body which in the opinion of the Minister is a body proper to make such an application;
(*b*) vehicles when standing or parked in places specially set aside for the purpose;
(*c*) vehicles drawn or propelled by hand, save as hereinafter provided.

(3) The Minister shall have power by regulations to add to, or vary, the requirements of this Act, and to require or permit distinctive lamps to be carried displaying lights of such colour and used under such conditions as may be prescribed in the case of—

(*a*) vehicles used as public service vehicles within the

meaning of this Act, or any class or description thereof or hackney carriages;

(*b*) vehicles used for naval, military, air force, or police purposes, or as ambulances, or for any other special purposes mentioned in the regulation or in the case of vehicles used for naval, military, or air force purposes to grant exemption (whole or partial) from the requirements of this Act;

and, where distinctive lamps are so required or permitted, to prohibit similar lamps being carried by any other vehicles.

. . . . . .

Section 12. Any regulations made under this Act shall be laid before both Houses of Parliament forthwith, and if an address is presented to His Majesty by either House of Parliament within the next subsequent twenty-eight days, on which that House has sat after any such regulation is laid before it praying that the regulation shall be annulled, it shall thenceforth be void, but without prejudice to the validity of anything previously done thereunder or to the making of a new regulation.

INDEX

THE END

www.ingramcontent.com/pod-product-compliance
Ingram Content Group UK Ltd.
Pitfield, Milton Keynes, MK11 3LW, UK
UKHW021905150926
475560UK00003B/190

9 780837 183893